Dr. Hannen writes a prescription for medical and professional healing, and then fills the prescription with clear and concise therapeutic formulas. He then gift wraps the prescription package in a biblical tapestry! The book is enlightening and very light to read!

—MIKE GUTMAN, M.D.
PAST PRESIDENT, FLORIDA PSYCHIATRIC SOCIETY

This is a refreshing book that brings both truth and light to the lives of those who read it. Dr. Hannen uses the wisdom from the past with the science of the present, blended with God's timeless laws to give Christians the knowledge they need to gain and maintain health. Only a clinician of his caliber would have the insight to guide one along the path to wellness that Dr. Hannen discusses.

—JOHN W. BRIMHALL, B.A., B.S., D.C., FIAMA, DIBAK
DEVELOPER, THE 10 STEPS TO WELLNESS PROGRAM
FOUNDER, BRIMHALL CHIROPRACTIC CLINIC

During the eight years that I have been privileged to pastor Dr. Scott Hannen, I have learned that his integrity is impeccable and his desire to "heal the sick" is his consuming passion. Dr. Scott Hannen is the only physician on earth that I completely trust.

—REV. DAVID PIZZIMENTI, PASTOR
GLORY TO HIM FELLOWSHIP CHURCH, OZARK, AL
HOST, *UNCHANGING WORD* TV BROADCAST

We are honored to recommend Dr. Scott Hannen's *Healing by Design.* Our professional and personal relationship has confirmed to us his strength of human compassion that comes from the heart of God for mankind. You will be challenged, but not overwhelmed; your mind will be stimulated to raise your level of health, but not shocked so that you give up. May you read, enjoy and grow into a new capacity for health.

—HARRY AND CHERYL SALEM
SALEM FAMILY MINISTRIES

Informative, practical and the "Rand McNally" for health and nutrition—this book definitely put me on the right road! As a cancer survivor, Dr. Hannen's book *Healing by Design* gets my vote. It is definitely a must-read!

—BILL AND RENEÉ MORRIS
RECORDING ARTISTS, COMPOSERS AND PRODUCERS

ACKNOWLEDGMENTS

To my loving wife, Aneesa, and my incredible son, Chas, for all the love and support given during the long hours you endured while I was completing this project.

To my parents and family who have always supported and never stopped believing in me.

To all of my friends and mentors who have made so many valuable deposits into my life.

To Stephen Strang and the entire team at Strang Communications who allowed me the opportunity to reach the masses with this message. From the deepest part of my heart, thank you, and may the blessings of God be upon you.

HEALING *by* DESIGN

DR. SCOTT HANNEN

SILOAM®
A STRANG COMPANY

HEALING BY DESIGN by Scott Hannen, D.C.
Published by Siloam
A Strang Company
600 Rinehart Road
Lake Mary, Florida 32746
www.siloam.com

Unless otherwise noted, all Scripture quotations are from the King James Version of the Bible.

Scripture quotations marked NIV are from the Holy Bible, New International Version. Copyright © 1973, 1978, 1984, International Bible Society. Used by permission.

Cover design by Eric Powell
Interior typography by Sallie Traynor

This book is not intended to provide medical advice or to take the place of medical advice and treatment from your personal physician. Readers are advised to consult their own doctors or other qualified health professionals regarding the treatment of their medical problems. Neither the publisher nor the author takes any responsibility for any possible consequences from any treatment, action or preparation to any person reading or following the information in this book. If readers are taking prescription medications, they should consult with their physicians and not take themselves off of medicines to start supplementation without the proper supervision of a physician.

Library of Congress Cataloging-in-Publication Data

Hannen, Scott.
  Healing by design / Scott Hannen.
     p. cm.
  ISBN 0-88419-949-5 (Trade Paper)
  1. Naturopathy. 2. Healing. 3. Health--Religious
aspects--Christianity. I. Title.
RZ440.H363 2003
615.5'35--dc21

                                        2003007006

03 04 05 06 07 — 87654
Printed in the United States of America

TABLE OF CONTENTS

INTRODUCTION

Understanding the wonder of human design is absolutely essential to learning to walk in the optimal health that God desires for you to enjoy. I have often used the analogy of caring for an automobile to explain our responsibility to learn to care for our body as God intended. If you put cheap gas into the tank of a fine automobile instead of high-octane gas, that beautiful machine will not function as it was intended. Learning to protect it from abuse and to maintain it through preventive maintenance is as vital to the optimal function of your car as learning to care for your body is necessary for its optimal function.

Taking responsibility for your health is not difficult, but it is necessary if you are to enjoy good health or if you need to restore health that has been compromised. While faith in God is essential for you to be able to receive healing and walk in the peace that promotes health, stewardship is also required to live in a way that does not abuse your body, knowingly or unknowingly, which allows sickness in the first place. Stewardship of your physical, mental and spiritual resources (your health) must be learned and practiced in order for you to enjoy the blessing of health that God promises.

Understanding the reality that God designed the body to have the ability to heal itself when given proper nutrition and care will give you the tools you need to walk in health and help your family to do the same. I want to recommend that you read this book with a prayerful attitude, asking the Holy Spirit to show you where you need to apply the wisdom that it contains and to empower you to make right choices that will fulfill the stewardship required for you to enjoy abundant health.

—Don Colbert, M.D.
Author of *Walking in Divine Health, Toxic Relief,* Bible Cure
Series and other best-selling books

PREFACE

T here are a wide variety of medical books on the market today that discuss many different facets of health and healing. Some books cover only the surgical and drug approaches to illness, which conventional medicine practices; others focus on nutrition, vitamin and mineral therapies, mind over matter and other self-care approaches. There are also books that examine the doctrine of divine healing, showing biblical principles that promise healing through faith and prayer alone.

This book focuses on several of these elements of healing that, as a skilled physician, I have personally witnessed and found to be effective for bringing healing to the body and for maintaining superior health. However, the focus of this book is a perspective of healthcare and healing that tends to go unrecognized by many, especially by those who have been trained in the popular, though faulty, philosophy that promises "a pill for every ill," sometimes resulting in people becoming victims of deception.

Health Education 101

Of all of the subjects I discuss with people, health seems to be the one people know the least about. Our society is filled with people who are highly "educated" about all kinds of sports, television personalities, hobbies, jobs, local and world events, and other less-impacting issues of life. I often wonder how many of these well-educated people could give correct answers to pass a ten-point quiz about basic health principles. I can guess their answers would be conflicting because there are so many different opinions about health issues presented by various approaches to healthcare.

This book is focused primarily on the way God designed our bodies and how He included natural mechanisms to restore and maintain our bodies in health. It will also expose problems to our health and show how people are led down the destructive path to sickness and disease. Biblical concepts of divine healing and faith are also briefly referenced to provide a broader understanding of God's design for our healing—body, soul and spirit.

A Sure Foundation

I have chosen to accept the Bible as a foundational reference for my life because its truths have stood the test of time. Although there have been many attempts of science to disprove biblical claims, in the end, science usually validates what the Bible teaches. Regarding health, God gave us principles of lifestyle to understand and practice that will help us maintain and restore health for our whole person. And He also promises to heal with His supernatural intervention, through faith and prayer.

If your belief system does not allow for divine healing, that is fine. Allow yourself to be open-minded, and, after reading this book, you might be willing to accept new truths when placed in their proper perspective. Rather than trying to convince you, I want to challenge you to take a closer look at why you believe what you do and to help you determine what you can expect the results of your belief system to be.

ELEMENTS OF DIVINE DESIGN

So God created man in his own image, in the image of God created he him; male and female created he them. And God blessed them, and God said unto them, Be fruitful, and multiply, and replenish the earth, and subdue it: and have dominion over the fish of the sea, and over the fowl of the air, and over every living thing that moveth upon the earth.

—GENESIS 1:27–28

CHAPTER 1

The Wonder of Human Design

The beginning verses of the Bible describe God's plan in Creation, revealing an elaborate and intricate design that should evoke wonder and awe in our hearts. God spoke the human body into existence. He made Adam with a divine design and for a specific function. Then He created Eve out of Adam to complement him in her own divine design and function. God created mankind—male and female—to have *dominion* over the entire earth and everything on it (Gen. 1:28). There was no compromise in the construction, no flaw in the design of God's ultimate creation—mankind. If we don't grasp this reality, it is easy to forget that we were not created for the earth; the earth was created for us.

The genetic patterns that have formed every person since that first man was created were considered in God's mind in conjunction with His master plan. All the provisions needed to sustain life as God ordained it were placed in the earth specifically for our use. We live on a planet—earth—that was tailor-made to suit our every need and desire. God equipped our bodies to live in the environment that He provided, and He even gave us the capability of adapting to changes in that environment.

For example, hair often grows faster in colder climates, seemingly attempting to maintain warmth. Sinuses produce more mucus in dry climates, and the circulatory system will adapt to higher altitudes that have lower oxygen levels. The ways the body's systems can adapt to the changing environmental demands are virtually endless.

During my years of clinical practice, I have observed many people experience severe traumas that left their bodies literally unrecognizable. During their healing process, through a barrage of bodily chemical reactions along with awesome new growth potential, I have watched their bodies miraculously reshape and regenerate into a normal structure in a matter of weeks or months. It is this wonder of the human design on which I have focused, to discover how it works and to understand the innate power for the body to heal itself that God created within every creature.

Of course, medical science may assist the body's healing process with some wonderful intervention (such as plastic surgery, for example), but it is the body doing the healing. No man has ever healed another man. Without the divine design in every human body to initiate healing, no physician could begin to assist in that process. There may be intervention through the wisdom and knowledge given to doctors, but the healing itself is either *divine* or *by design*. *Either way, as far as I am concerned, God gets the credit.* Health is God's business; it is His loving desire for every creature.

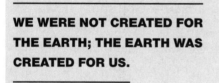

WE WERE NOT CREATED FOR THE EARTH; THE EARTH WAS CREATED FOR US.

My "Health" Story

I have not always appreciated the divine design of our bodies or understood that God wanted us to enjoy abundant health. Like many people, I was trained to believe that when people talked about health or sickness, they were just talking about what was happening to a physical structure—a skeleton with organs placed inside of it, and with some veins, some arteries, a brain and a nervous system. In my naive mind, I pictured skin stretched over that structure and filled with blood that allowed us to exist. In my ignorance, I thought that as we went about life we would contact "things" out there—things like viruses, bacteria and "bugs" that would make us sick. I pictured them moving around, interchanging between people and transferring from one to another.

I thought that when one of those bugs (microorganisms) got on you, it would get inside your body and make you sick or give you some type of disease. Then you would go to your doctor and he would give you a pill, because there was a pill to kill every bug. As long as you took the right pill for the right bug, you would be OK, and the symptoms would go away.

Of course, you never wanted to get one of the bad bugs inside of you, because then its name got a little longer and it was harder to pronounce when the doctor gave you the diagnosis. It seemed like the longer that word was and the harder it was to pronounce, the sicker you would get. It also seemed that sometimes pills wouldn't work when you got that big bug, so then you gave it all you had—out of desperation, you even prayed.

If it was really bad, and you got a diagnosis that called your bug *incurable*, your only hope was miraculous intervention—a divine touch from God—or you were going to die, since medical intervention couldn't help you. This may be the way you were also taught to believe concerning sickness and healthcare.

As a child subject to this healthcare "system," it seemed I was continually suffering from some kind of "bug." I was one of the sickest kids in the county. When I was four years old, I almost died with spinal meningitis. I had my appendix taken out and my tonsils removed. And, in what seemed at least a monthly event, I would have a throat infection, an ear infection or some type of infection. In other words, if something was going around, I was always the first in line to "catch" it.

I was so rarely free from symptoms that I seemed frail because of constant sickness. My parents were following the suggestions of the current medical system as I have described it—a system that gave you a pill for every ill. I would just keep taking those pills to kill those bugs, and sometimes I would feel better and sometimes it would seem as if the pills weren't doing anything to help. My mother would continue giving them to me anyway, and in a week or two I would get over whatever I had, whether or not the pills were working.

I did not understand then what I know now about the awesome design of the body to heal itself. I did not have the benefit of medical training or any understanding of God's Word; I was only taught what conventional medicine prescribed and what my family accepted as "normal." As a result, without my family realizing it, I was being robbed of the health God wanted me to have. Now I understand that anytime we are being robbed or are experiencing any destruction of our health, there is always hope for finding the cure as long as we align our thoughts and actions with a reliable source of truth that provides correct instruction on how to activate the body's built-in healing potential.

HEALING ITSELF IS EITHER DIVINE OR BY DESIGN.

A light dawns

For most of my teenage years and all of my adult life, I have been motivated by a strong internal drive in a quest for truth about how our bodies work and why they sometimes get sick. The reason I suffered so many health problems in my youth was because I wasn't receiving correct information from a reliable source of truth. In my search for truth regarding healing and health, I was trying to gain wisdom and knowledge from a conventional medical system that is strongly motivated by the amount of money it can generate rather than focusing on the needs of sick people. It seemed the more I followed that approach to health, the sicker I became.

During my first years of graduate studies, I stumbled into some biblical principles for health, though at the time I still did not know these truths were in the Bible. I just knew that they were different from the medical "wisdom" currently being taught. At that time, I was ignorant in my knowledge of God's system of healing; I didn't know that there was any other system of healthcare than the conventional system to which I had been exposed. I didn't know that the Bible contained sound foundational health principles that instruct us in ways to cooperate with the healing potential that is inherent to the human design. I was just convinced that there must be a better way of taking care of your health than I was currently practicing, because it wasn't working for me.

Do you know who first introduced me to another way? People like my grandmother and my great-grandmother who would say things like, "No, son; don't take that drug. Take this natural remedy I am giving you." Although it usually seemed pretty crazy to me, when I gave in and took their alternative, I would see good results.

Now, I admit that some of their remedies were often rough on me. But whatever they did—whether it was placing a big poultice on my chest that smelled strong enough to chase demons, dogs or anything else away, or giving me a dose of salts, black draw or cod liver oil that would keep me close to the bathroom—somehow when I finished their "treatments," my sickness would be gone. As I got older, I started comparing the people who followed the doctors' prescribed "drug" system and those who, like my grandmothers, used natural remedies to see who lived the longest.

I discovered that people who followed the "drug" system didn't live as long as those who stayed away from doctors and used more natural "medicines." If they did live to be seventy or eighty, their quality of life was so poor that it seemed as if they had died at around age fifty; they were merely "existing," not living life to the fullest. From that point, they were just prisoners in bondage to medications, hospital and doctor visits and decisions as to which specialist they needed to see next.

I observed people like my grandparents and great-grandparents who lived long, productive and active lives. For example, my great-grandmother lived to be one hundred three years old. I remember the doctors sending letters to her, warning her that she needed to come in for a checkup. The only time I was ever aware that she had a doctor's visit was the day she was born and the day she was pronounced dead. She was very outspoken; she would often tell us that she didn't trust most doctors and that she wouldn't let them scare her into going to their office. Of course, you may think this skeptical attitude finally ended her life. And it did—at one hundred three years of age, still maintaining her dignity, my great-grandmother went to be with the Lord. She had maintained her connection to the divine design that allowed her body to maintain health for over a century.

My other grandparents, as well as my wife's grandparents, lived well into their eighties. When I say "lived," I mean they were healthy and active until their death. My wife's grandmother even chopped wood in her latter years. They were all still carrying in wood, hanging laundry outside, cooking and doing all of the things that they enjoyed doing as a part of their vigorous lifestyle. Maybe their alternatives weren't so crazy after all.

Even before I became a doctor, I observed friends whom I had not seen for several years, and I realized their health was rapidly deteriorating. They were either bent over or their faces were drawn and emaciated and their hair didn't look healthy. Some had a blank stare on their face and moved at about half speed in a weakened state of lethargy.

When I asked them what had happened to them, their story went something like this: "Well, I went in for a checkup, and the doctor told me I had _____" (they would spit out the ten dollar word—whatever it was, something like "_____algia" or "_____itis"). Then, of course, they would continue, "The doctor gave me some pills to take, but they caused another problem, so he gave me another pill to fix the problem the first pill caused…" and on and on they would go. These people got to carry their little bag of medication around, though their health continued to deteriorate dramatically in a very short period of time.

Medical science does much good

Please let me clarify, emphatically, that *I am not anti-medical or against the obvious good that conventional medical science can do!* Yes, there is obviously a time and a place and a purpose for prescribed medications and for surgeries. The problem, as I see it, is that many times conventional medicine is trying to fix everything using drugs and surgery without addressing root causes of disease.

Simple observation of people would indicate that there must be something that healthy people are doing correctly, because they are getting better results. I guessed that part of the answer was the commonsense approach of my grandparents, the old-timers' remedies and the way they believed.

Taking Personal Responsibility

I now recognize the hand of God creating the interest and directing my observations and conclusions about a natural approach to health. Those observations and conclusions resulted in my pursuing alternative methods of healing that friends and family around me thought were ridiculous. I researched many of the "old-timers'" remedies

THE PROBLEM IS THAT CONVENTIONAL MEDICINE IS TRYING TO FIX *EVERYTHING* USING DRUGS AND SURGERY.

and studied what they believed about health. I concluded that if people and cultures had existed for thousands of years without our modern-day drugs, which have existed for only the last one hundred years or so, common sense alone would suggest there might be another approach to health than just "taking a pill for every ill."

Another observation that guided my thinking came from my clinical studies. I would study scientific journals and read, "This product is the cure!" A few months later I would read in those same journals, "We've reevaluated our studies and find serious side effects and less than conclusive evidence that this product is a cure." From that I concluded something was amiss. I wondered, *What about all of those poor people who followed the recommendations given in the first study?* Sadly, I knew the answer—they are now called statistics, meaning that many of them either suffered ill effects and recovered or perhaps were no longer with us.

Even with all the technological achievements and wonder drugs the conventional medical system offers today, statistics still say that the three most likely causes of your death will be:

1. Heart disease
2. Cancer
3. Stroke

So if you do nothing different from the average American lifestyle you are now living, those are the three most likely ways you will exit the planet, according to the National Center for Health Statistics.[1] How does that make you feel? Unfortunately, that is the best we have been able to produce from the most advanced medical and scientific community with the best technology in the world.

As I focused my studies on the deteriorating health of the general population, I became more convinced that we need to return to the original plan of the Creator, who designed our bodies to live in health and placed within them the power of healing. We need to learn how to become responsible for the personal care of the divine design of our bodies, which the apostle Paul referred to as "the temple[s] of God" (1 Cor. 3:16). That doesn't mean we must eliminate medical science, as I have stated. But we are placing an unfair burden on physicians and even researchers to expect them to insure health when we are not being responsible with the incredible body God designed for us.

> COMMON SENSE ALONE WOULD SUGGEST THERE MIGHT BE ANOTHER APPROACH TO HEALTH THAN JUST "TAKING A PILL FOR EVERY ILL."

Sick Christians

As I began to speak in churches throughout the country and share the simple truths of health I was practicing in my clinic, my wife and I were appalled to find that church people—sincere Christians—were as sick as the unchurched people I see in my clinic. We began to realize that most of the churches we visited have one big thing in common that startled us. They are *full* of sick people—very sick people!

This reality hit me full force because it was so contrary to God's promises of abundant life and healing for His people. The way I understand the Bible is that Christ died to take eternal damnation from us and that the stripes on His back were for our physical healing as well. What I saw in the churches was sickness instead of healing, and that confused me. The Word of God has promised a covenant of healing to the believer, and yet our churches are filled with sick people.

This really bothered me, so I started asking the Lord about it in my prayer and study time. God began to reveal to me divine principles that affect our physical well-being, which have changed the way I live and the way I practice in my clinic. I began to understand more clearly the things that people are doing that make them sick. The sad thing is that most people, including pastors and Christian leaders, have no idea why this is happening to them.

Many pastors have taught the truth of divine healing to their congregations, building faith in their hearts that God wants them to be in health and that we can pray and believe for healing. Pastors have persistently taught the mechanics of faith, which are all necessary to good theology. However, many have not taught the personal responsibility we have to take care of the body God has given us, based on the way He designed us to live.

To get the results from God's promises that you desire, you must simply obey the Word—all of it. The Bible cannot be approached like eating from a buffet. You can't just pick and choose what you want and leave the rest behind. To achieve health and maintain it, you have to follow biblical principles regarding caring for your body, mind and spirit. The way you add supernatural results to your healthcare is to follow the instructions of the supernatural training manual—the Bible—regarding godly ways to maintain your body.

A common scenario

People are often confused between practicing their faith to receive healing and using medicine for a cure. It is humorous, sometimes, when we see ourselves in other people's actions. For example, a person comes to church and starts worshiping; he (or she) is having a good time, but suddenly begins to feel a little tightness in his throat. Soon it becomes hard to swallow, and the throat becomes sore. He tapes a healing scripture on the mirror and begins confessing the promises of God to heal. Later in the day he begins to be feverish, and his glands are even more swollen. Then he decides to go to the doctor to get a pill—the right pill for the right bug.

When he returns home, he declares, "I'm not going to take these, but I will have them just in case…" So he continues doing this thing that he calls "faith," confessing the promises of God to heal. By nightfall, the fever has become worse, and he is worried that he may have a bad bug that won't respond to the pill he has, and therefore he might need more medication. If that doesn't work, he might have to go to the hospital, and the fear continues to grow. So he takes the antibiotic he received, which does not affect viral bugs anyway, and he recovers in a few days, giving credit to the medication and to God.

Many people, including Christians, do not understand the divine design of their bodies in the way that the body fights illness. For example, they don't realize that fever is a sign that the body is trying to burn out an infection or viral "bug." And they don't understand why their body contracted the illness in the first place. When we violate the health needs of our bodies by our lifestyle choices, we get sick—it is that simple. We will discuss in detail in the next chapter how this happens. In our culture, we have been taught that when we get sick, doctors can give us relief with a pill. Or we resort to surgery to remove the diseased part, such as the appendix, tonsils or gallbladder.

Did you know that God doesn't make spare parts? Even medical science, which has advocated removing certain "unnecessary" parts such as tonsils, is discovering that people who keep all their parts have a better chance for living a healthy life. The overriding philosophy that says we can live any way we want to live, and then when we make ourselves sick the doctor will "fix" it by removing parts or giving us new parts or more pills is a violation of God's laws. We need to take personal responsibility to care for our body's divine design.

The sin problem

When Adam and Eve sinned in the Garden of Eden, they were separated from God, and the effects of sin entered into the world. Although the spiritual arrangements were altered, God did not change the way the body was created or its requirements for maintaining health. Man was still created to subdue, conquer and have dominion over all of the earth, including his own body. (See Genesis 1:28.)

What did change, sadly, is that the beautifully created body of Adam no longer had the relationship with God that gave him wisdom to live, allowing him to enjoy supernatural health all the time. I believe Adam and Eve constantly walked in a state of healing and dominion before they suffered the separation of their relationship with God. After that, they were on their own, though God graciously reached out to mankind continually, as the Old Testament teaches, still intent on giving them guidelines and safeguards to help them secure a healthy lifestyle.

Unfortunately, through thousands of years of separation from God, man has developed systems of life and healing that are not based on the Word of God. As a matter of fact, when I began to read medical journals and textbooks, I learned that much of today's approach to healing and health is atheistic; it doesn't recognize God at all. This is a reality that most Christians do not like to face. They want to live according to their comfortable lifestyle, and if they get sick, they will trust their health to a physician because they don't want to take responsibility for their health. Or they will call on the pastor to pray for them and expect instant healing through practicing their faith. If these methods fail to restore their health, they can then blame the physician or the pastor.

While I believe in both medical science and faith for healing, I am aware that it is ignorance of the divine design of our bodies that causes much sickness to begin with. It is my hope and prayer that as you gain understanding of the way God made your body, with built-in defense mechanisms and the innate ability to heal itself, you will begin to take personal responsibility for your health. As you do, you will find natural and supernatural ways to restore health and improve it, and you will learn to walk in divine health through following the laws of God the Creator, who designed you for that abundant life.

The wonder of a baby

Have you ever looked at a beautiful baby without feeling a sense of wonder in your heart for the marvelous way this tiny, perfect human being was formed? The psalmist referred to this wonder when he wrote:

> I will praise thee; for I am fearfully and wonderfully made: marvellous are thy works; and that my soul knoweth right well. My substance was not hid from thee, when I was made in secret, and curiously wrought in the lowest parts of the earth. Thine eyes did see my substance, yet being unperfect; and in thy book all my members were written, which in continuance were fashioned, when as yet there was none of them.
>
> —PSALM 139:14–16

Did you know that a baby begins as one cell and, when completely formed, contains approximately 100 trillion cells without any outside intervention except for the nutrients it receives from its mother? Isn't it amazing that heart tissue forms a heart and knows where it needs to be placed in the chest cavity? And isn't it amazing that one leg grows as long as the other, one arm grows as long as the other, and one eye works together with the other eye? How about the fact that all of the senses such as hearing, sight, taste, smell and mental awareness can put it all together, through sensory integration, so that the baby can communicate accurately with the world?

Medical science still has not been able to understand or completely describe the wonder of human reproduction. Neither have they been able to duplicate it. They can replicate by attempting to work with what's already there (DNA, genomes and so forth), and they can try to manipulate the elements of life they have separated, but *neither physicians nor scientists can create life.*

The Creator of life who designed the body, mind and spirit has not been replaced by medical science—with Him alone lie the secrets of creation. And He designed the body to heal itself as well. As part of its maintenance of life, right now your body is multiplying its red blood cells at such a rate that in three months you will have all new red blood cells. In one year, all of your cells will be completely exchanged for new ones. The only things that will be left are the DNA patterns inside of those cells that make you *you*. Even the actual material in the DNA will also be exchanged for new material. Isn't that incredible?

As you sit reading this book, your skin cells are sloughing off. Perhaps you have noticed that when you shower every day, you leave some hair behind. If the body was not reproducing new skin and hair, you would be "skinless" and bald in a few weeks. Instead, you probably spend

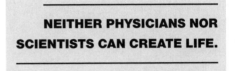

NEITHER PHYSICIANS NOR SCIENTISTS CAN CREATE LIFE.

time trying to tan your skin and spend big bucks at the hair salon to get your hair cut. You have healthy skin and a healthy head of hair because of the body's ability to reproduce itself. Your nails also keep growing and requiring you to manicure them if you are healthy.

Did you know that when you were in the womb as a tiny cell, trying to survive through conception, the bacteria, viruses, parasites and other destructive elements in your mother's body were trying to get to you? They did not succeed because you were a tiny seed of life, given by the Creator, and you were conquering the destructive forces around you. No wonder the psalmist David declared to God: "I will praise thee; for I am fearfully and wonderfully made: marvellous are thy works; and that my soul knoweth right well" (Ps. 139:14).

In the following chapters we will explore this wonder that God designed to become a human being. Of course, we understand that He made us more than just a body—we are body, soul and spirit. These areas of our life all affect each other and must be properly cared for to allow health to flow synergistically through the body, the soul and the spirit.

CHAPTER 2

How Do We Get Sick?

Thomas Edison, who lived in the late nineteenth century, made a very prophetic statement regarding healthcare:

> The doctor of the future will give no medicine, but will interest his patients in the care of the human frame, in diet, and in the cause and prevention of disease.

When a person gets sick, he usually tries to find something to make him *feel* better. Most people do not think of *curing the sickness*; instead, they usually seek *relief from the symptoms*. Very seldom does a person who is ill search for the cause of his problem—that seems irrelevant because he is distracted by his immediate pain and suffering.

For example, a person who gets a stuffy head with sinus pain, watery eyes and headache will probably take Tylenol, aspirin or one of the dozens of cold remedies that can be purchased over the counter. It would be unusual for that person to try to locate the source of these symptoms. Most people are happy just to take a medication and be free from the discomfort, which makes them believe they are getting better.

This treatment approach to symptoms of illness may give short-term benefits, but it can also create long-term problems. Let me explain. When your nose begins to run and sinuses begin to drain, it is a signal that your body is cleansing itself. It is trying to remove or flush out uninvited invaders—antigens such as chemicals, dust, pollen and microorganisms—by flushing them out of the body through mucus to prevent them from entering the lungs and then the bloodstream. In this way the body is working to heal itself.

Unfortunately, this cleansing process makes a person feel "sick." So instead of allowing the body to rid itself of these invaders, we take "medicines" that give relief from the uncomfortable symptoms that accompany it. The medications dry the membranes, getting rid of the stuffy nose, but in doing so, they allow the invaders to enter the lung where they are immediately absorbed into the blood stream. This process allows the invaders to penetrate the system more deeply than they normally would if the body was allowed to fight them.

> **MOST PEOPLE DO NOT THINK OF *CURING THE SICKNESS*; INSTEAD, THEY USUALLY SEEK *RELIEF FROM THE SYMPTOMS*.**

After spreading throughout the system, the invaders have better access to damage the vital internal structures and organs and to deposit themselves in the tissues of the body. When a buildup of these invaders overloads the system, it can result in a variety of problems—such as allergies, arthritis and a damaged immune system. Heavy metal and chemical buildups in the body, for example, have been shown to produce autoimmune reactions (such as lupus and rheumatoid arthritis).

Masking the pain can cause the overuse of injured joints, which can cause further damage. With the continual use of anti-inflammatory medications (ibuprofen, acetaminophen) to relieve pain, the brain does not register further damage that leads to degeneration of the joints. In the same way, headache medications may cover up symptoms that could be warning signs of an underlying cause (such as stroke, aneurysm, tumors or high blood pressure). Antacids (such as Tums or Rolaids) neutralize stomach acid and reduce heartburn without treating the more serious digestive problems. And calcium needs stomach acid in order to break down for absorption. People taking antacids for their source of calcium are neutralizing the stomach acid necessary to break down the calcium, so it simply passes through the body.

You Can't Win a Bug War

Bacteria, viruses, yeast, parasites and other microorganisms are constantly invading our bodies. These bugs are dispersed throughout most of our cells. If bugs were the cause of sickness, we would all be dead. The reason we are not overtaken is because the immune system keeps the bugs from overwhelming our system. There are ways bugs can multiply and cause an imbalance, leading to sickness and infection. Most people are trained to take an antibiotic if they get an infection. Is there another option? Consider these principles.

Principle 1

If I place a pile of garbage on the floor and leave it there, what do you suppose will happen in a couple of weeks? That's right; bugs will find it. I can go down to the store, get some bug spray and use it on the bugs, and they will die. But if I leave the garbage there another two weeks, what happens? More bugs! I can spray them again, and they will die. I can continue this "bug-killing" process repeatedly, getting rid of the bugs each time, or I can just simply get rid of the garbage and the bugs will disappear.

Principle 2

If water sits outside in a bucket for several days, bugs will infest it. I can spray bug spray in the bucket, and it will kill the bugs. But what happens in a few weeks? More bugs! Isn't it easier just to dump the bucket and fill it with fresh water? The law of stagnation promotes bug growth.

From these simple analogies, we can learn important principles for health. For example, if fluid "stagnates" in the sinus, you get a sinus infection. If it builds up in your ear, you get an ear infection. If it lodges in your lung, you get a lung infection (pneumonia).

Wherever you get stagnation from lack of flow of body fluids, you are prone to infection. In order to stop an infection, you need to "dump the bucket," or get the stagnated fluids moving and get rid of the garbage.

How Antibiotics Work

God created a body that was designed to win against any attack. The reason you are not dead now is that your immune system is fighting off all the bacteria, viruses, yeast, parasites and other microorganisms that are attacking it. It was designed with indescribable protection systems with which it arms itself against an attack, as well as a monitoring (intelligence) system that constantly evaluates every cell for its potential need for help. Whether the cell needs feeding, cleansing or protection, the body is on ready alert to make the delivery.

There are so many healing potentials locked away inside the body that man has yet to explore them all. Though science has defined the body parts and many of its systems, it still does not understand what generates that internal empowering force that we call *life*. Doctors may realize by observation what occurs in the body's chemistry, but they have no idea the mechanisms by which the body organizes and generates the hidden internal healing powers.

Science has spent most of its research dollars trying to figure out what generates these inherent recuperative powers so that they can control and direct these healing body processes. Their remedies try to direct and redirect the body's signals. For example, when someone gets a fever and begins to feel bad, it is because the body is generating heat to create an environment in which germs cannot survive. Many times the body will begin eliminating harmful invading germs by increasing secretions. A runny nose is a good example of this kind of elimination. Often a person will shiver (chills) to generate even more heat. This makes the person feels bad, forcing him to lie down and rest so the body can reserve its energy to fight off this attack, instead of working, playing or walking around.

After sleeping, the person's sinuses often drain into the back of the throat where the lymph glands begin trapping the germs. This causes them to swell. Some of the fluids may drain into the airways, causing the person to cough to remove the mucus. While all of these symptoms are happening, the body's internal system is producing antibodies. Much like a laboratory, the body produces antibodies, or immunity chemicals, to use as weapons against the invading army. It codes and labels each specific strain of germ attacking, and it develops its own specific immunity against it. These codes are processed and filed away so that the next time these particular strains try to attack the body, it will already have the right weapons developed so that, many times, if they show up again, the immune system can eliminate them before they are able to produce symptoms. We call this amazing process *acquired immunity*.

Let's look once more at the effect of what is taking place. The body has handled every circumstance and has set up the proper defenses to insure a victorious battle. No one had to train the body to do this. No man had to intervene and make the body fight. These defenses were in the original design. These mechanisms have kept humans alive since the beginning of time; they are time tested and proven.

In contrast to this natural healing process, the way our generation handles illness is quite different. There is very little regard for the body's ability to heal itself. Conventional medical wisdom says that chemicals heal, not the body. Pills make you feel better, therefore giving you a "sure" cure. What is wrong with this approach? To answer this question, let's revisit our sick person's scenario.

Someone develops a fever, chills, runny nose and sore throat with swollen glands, and a severe cough. Most people immediately take an aspirin or Tylenol to break the fever and stop the chills. This medication thwarts the body's ability to generate the heat that the body requires to fight the germs. Next, the person takes an antihistamine (cold medicine), and the sinus membranes dry up. This treatment allows invading germs and other harmful substances to enter into the lungs and go directly into the bloodstream, affecting the whole body. Because the glands are swollen, an antibiotic is usually prescribed. Once the antibiotic enters the system, the body's natural immunity has been overridden. Therefore, when the body produces a surge of antibodies to fight the immediate attack, no immunity is developed, so the immune system is actually weakened.

Finally, the person takes cough medication to stop the annoying cough. When this occurs, the body is unable to remove the accumulative fluids and mucus through expulsion. These fluids provide an excellent place for microorganisms to grow, which may produce infections in the lungs. The prescribed antibiotic may defeat a bacterial microorganism from spreading into the lungs, but not a virus. Antibiotics have no effect on viral microorganisms. And there are many bacteria today that are resistant to antibiotics as well, which could very well produce a bronchial or lung infection such as pneumonia, even while the person is taking the antibiotic.

Now, let's make it personal. You get a fever, chills, runny nose, a sore throat with swollen glands and a severe cough. You feel bad. The body is producing all these symptoms as part of a healing process, which will also make you stronger for the next fight. If you take a variety of drugs to block the body's attempt to heal itself, whose side are you on?

A Balanced Body

The body is a well-balanced, biomechanically efficient structure. If that balance is altered for any reason, the body becomes mechanically disadvantaged, creating imbalances that cause structures to shift in order to compensate for the imbalance. In other words, you get sick.

So many people today are suffering needlessly. They suffer from joint restrictions, muscle tightness, spasms, lack of mobility and a variety of other pain syndromes. Many continue to look for relief from a pill or other drug formula. What most people do not consider is the fact that none of these "remedies" address the cause of their illness.

This process for getting sick is much like a stack of bricks that shifts when one brick at the bottom of the stack is moved. When these shifts create imbalance inside the body, the joints are placed under pressure and stress, which produces friction. The result is that the joints start to break down and degenerate. Medical science calls this phenomenon *degenerative joint disease* (DJD), as if some germ had entered the body and started chewing on the joints. A more common name is osteoarthritis (OA).

Perhaps the following analogy will help to clarify what happens when the body suffers imbalance. If the front end of your car gets out of alignment, what happens? It begins to cause the tread on your tires to wear unevenly. Why? Because the misalignment causes uneven stress on the tires, producing friction and uneven wear and tear on the tires. If you do not realign the car, even further damage can occur. The human body can be affected by misalignment in the same way. Our body is a marvelous biomechanical structure that consists of levers (bones), pulleys and cables (tendons and ligaments), and cushions (joints, disks and cartilage), which, if maintained properly in balance, make for a "smooth ride."

Another helpful analogy to understanding the body's balance is a pulley system, which can be quite effective for hoisting heavy objects as long as the rope stays in place in the pulley. If the rope slips off the pulley, the task becomes much more difficult because the mechanical advantage is lost. When using a lever to move a heavy object, the lever sets on a fulcrum, much like a seesaw. If it is placed at the correct leverage point, the tool is extremely efficient. What happens if the fulcrum shifts? Once again, you lose mechanical advantage. Once mechanical advantage is lost, the result is uneven or accentuated pressure.

When body parts are in constant motion and they lose their mechanical advantage, increased friction and pressure result. Increasing friction and pressure cause structures to break down, or degenerate. This kind of degeneration is occurring in the bodies of many people, yet they are completely unaware of the concept of imbalance or degeneration. They often visit my clinic with symptoms like those mentioned previously, but mostly with pain. Many have been hurting for years.

If you have never had severe pain, you cannot imagine how it affects a person mentally. I have seen people take drastic measures, even submitting to radical surgical procedures and medications with strong side effects, in an effort to eliminate chronic pain. Patients often tell me how many physicians, therapies and treatments they have tried, all without finding relief. Some even have permanent injuries as a result of their previous treatments. They could have been spared all of that if they understood how the body is designed and learned to cooperate with it to let it heal itself.

Understanding diagnosis

When a person goes to a doctor because the joints in his hands are inflamed and painful, the doctor examines the joints and runs tests. When the patient returns at a later visit to get the results of the tests, the doctor looks over the test results and says, "We found that you have arthritis." The person readily replies, "I knew it!" There seems to be a sense of satisfaction in people when they get a specific diagnosis. Probably pain medication is prescribed, and the patient is sent home with a diagnosis and a prescription. What is wrong with this picture?

Let us break it down, using arthritis as an example. First, you have inflamed and painful joints in your hands. You know you have it. No one needs to report this to you. If you go to the doctor for a diagnosis and he tells you that you have inflamed, painful joints, you would probably say, "I knew that. That's why I came to see you." If he calls it arthritis, he is only using a Latin word (*arth*, which means joint, and *itis*, which means inflamed) that means "inflamed joints." You have just paid your doctor a few hundred doctors to convert the name of your symptoms into Latin. The obvious question is left unanswered: "How did I get sick?"

How about fibromyalgia? You go to the doctor because you have chronic muscle tightness and pain, usually across the neck, shoulders and upper back. The doctor runs expensive tests and returns with the diagnosis: fibromyalgia. Guess what *fibromyalgia* means? *Fibro* comes from fibrous, which means "containing fibers."[1] In lay terms it could be described as tight and ropy-feeling muscles. The next part of the word is *my*, meaning "muscle." And the last part of the word, *algia*, means "painful condition." So basically, *fibromyalgia* simply means "tight, ropy-feeling muscles that are in pain."

Didn't you already know that before you went to the doctor's appointment? You were there because you had tight, ropy-feeling muscles that were causing you pain. Once again, the physician was paid to translate the symptoms into medical language and, hopefully, prescribe something to relieve symptoms. This type of diagnosis is called *symptom diagnosis.*

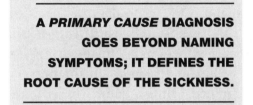

A *PRIMARY CAUSE* DIAGNOSIS GOES BEYOND NAMING SYMPTOMS; IT DEFINES THE ROOT CAUSE OF THE SICKNESS.

The symptoms that doctors are diagnosing are usually described with a word ending in *-itis* or *-algia*. People receive these types of symptom diagnoses every day, sometimes taking great comfort that the doctor has located their problem and expecting that to mean they are on the quick road to recovery. The fact is, no primary cause for the symptoms has been named, just the symptoms themselves. Again, this question remains unanswered: "How did I get sick?"

A *primary cause* diagnosis goes beyond naming symptoms; it defines the root cause of the sickness. For example, a primary cause would be something like fracture, dislocation or spinal subluxation. It is important not to be sidetracked with a symptom diagnosis, which fails to identify the underlying cause of your illness. There is an underlying cause that must be found in order for the physician to accurately assist the body in its efforts to heal itself.

One of the first things I tell my patients is, "I do not treat symptoms." I do not treat "disorders" by whatever name: fibromyalgia, lupus, arthritis, chronic fatigue or any other named malady. However, I do treat a lot of individuals who have been *diagnosed* with these conditions. Instead of treating their symptomatic disorder, I treat the body to assist it in its fight to restore a normal balance to the entire system. My goal is to unlock the body's potential to heal itself.

I have treated patients diagnosed with arthritis and fibromyalgia who had multiple structural, as well as nutrient, imbalances, which caused their muscles and joints to experience pressure and friction, causing pain. In this case, the first answer to their symptoms is to realign the structure (which is a primary cause), using natural methods, to unlock the joints and set them back into their proper alignment. The second answer is to supplement their deficiencies with specific nutrients. This alleviates the joint distress that is causing them to be inflamed, and it relaxes the muscles.

Muscles spasm when the nerves that connect to them become irritated. Joints inflame when friction is produced in that joint or if uneven pressures are applied to the joint, creating irritation. Patients have visited my clinic because of chronic knee pain for which they have been taking arthritis drugs and having cortisone injections, which do provide temporary relief but cause further destruction of the joints in the long run. After examining them, I almost always observe a weight shift to the side of the painful knee.

I then explain to them that the knees are supposed to evenly disperse the body weight between them. When one knee carries more weight than the other, the knee becomes irritated, which is soon followed by muscle and joint pain along with inflammation. Although the pain is experienced in the knee, most of the correction that needs to be done is in the pelvic area. Once we shift the pelvis back to the center so that the weight redistributes evenly between the knees, the knee pain usually disappears, sometimes immediately. I tell my patients that I have to put on my "body mechanic" outfit so I can give them a "front-end alignment." They appreciate the humor, especially after suffering so long with pain that disappears in so short a time.

A Lesson in Biomechanics

If you understand basic functions of your divine design, you can understand how you get sick and learn to live in such a way that you avoid much pain caused by misusing or abusing your body. To that end, allow me to give you a simple lesson in biomechanics. You may be aware that the brain and spinal cord are the vital structures of the central nervous system, which runs the entire body. They are housed and protected by the skull, seven cervical vertebrae (neck), twelve thoracic vertebrae (mid back), five lumbar vertebrae and the sacrum/coccyx (tailbone). All combine together to make up one single spinal column.

Nerves of the spinal cord exit the spinal column through holes in the vertebrae (called *neural foramina*). As these nerves branch off the spinal cord at different levels of the spinal column, they are then referred to as the *peripheral nervous system*. These nerves connect to the various body organs, limbs, muscles and so forth. The two main categories of nerves are *sensory* and *motor*. Sensory nerves are responsible for telling the brain what we feel (for example, heat, cold, pain or touch). Motor nerves deliver responses from the brain and spinal cord to the body parts that allow us to move and function, such as flexing muscles, moving arms, walking and bending.

Nerves are highly sensitive to pressure, so when the structures around the nerves (vertebrae) get shifted out of alignment, they stimulate the nerves, which respond with a sometimes unpleasant sensation. Think back to when you dissected frogs in your high school biology lab. Remember how the frog's legs would jump or contract when you poked the muscles in its legs? The stimulus of your poking caused the muscles to react. Likewise, stimulating nerves in the wrong way causes painful muscle spasms in our body.

If our posture shifts out of alignment, it stimulates the nerve receptors, and the muscles tighten up. I see many patients who suffer from chronic pain syndrome and experience this phenomenon. These patients do not need conventional medications to relieve their pain; they need a primary cause diagnosis that finds where pressure is firing the muscles into spasms so that it can be "fixed" and the muscles can relax as normal. This treatment will not only alleviate pain, but it will also prevent further possibilities of damage and help avoid further problems.

The pelvis is the body's platform. The legs attach into the pelvis on each side, supporting the rest of the body. The tailbone is the foundation upon which the spine rests. The shoulder is attached at the neck and the mid back, and it works much like a string puppet.

When the hip tilts one way, the shoulder tilts the other to keep us from tipping over. The head is attached on top of the neck and maintains the center of gravity, or the center of balance. The shoulders balance to the hip, and the head tries to maintain the center.

If the weight shifts off of this delicate midline balance in any direction—forward, backward or to either side—even the slightest uneven weight disbursement will create irritation or overstimulation, which can cause pain, inflammation and eventually a wide variety of other health conditions if left undetected.

There are three main ways the body shifts off of the midline:

1. Twists, called *torsion*
2. Leans to one side, called *lateral shift*
3. Leans forward or backward, called *A-P shift*

Usually when the posture is out of balance it is because of a trauma, perhaps hitting the head, falling, running into something, stumbling, sleeping wrong or generally poor postural habits, to name a few. There is usually a combination of the three shifts in the spinal column—torsion, lateral and A-P—depending upon the area involved and what the type of trauma is. When someone visits my clinic for examination and treatment, whatever his or her symptoms are, I first like to evaluate the musculoskeletal system, understanding that it is responsible to protect the nervous system.

Because the brain and nervous system act as "mission control," I like to know that all contact is clearly established between the brain, the nervous system and the body parts before I start making a diagnosis. What most people fail to realize is that the nerves that allow us to feel, move, touch and perform other normal activities are the same nerves that allow the function of vital organs like our heart, liver and kidneys. People many times have organ problems because of nerve deficiencies. In other words, the brain cannot properly communicate with the organ, the organ's needs cannot be satisfied, so the function of the organ begins to degenerate.

By simply removing this nerve interference (aligning the shifted structure), we can restore the communication to the organ, which allows the organ to thrive and to heal. That is why you may have heard of people who, after receiving chiropractic adjustments, have been healed of kidney disease, ulcers, chronic stomach problems, bladder conditions and other serious ailments. It is overwhelming to realize the number of people who have structural misalignments that are creating biomechanical disadvantage, restricted movement, subluxations and so forth and producing sickness, pain, inflammation and other symptoms for which they do not understand the primary cause. Subluxation is often called the silent killer.

The two leading causes of pain in America are:

1. Headache
2. Low back pain

Thousands of Americans suffer with muscle tension and mechanical headaches (headaches produced from musculoskeletal imbalances and nerve irritation) because of chronic misalignments that continually pull at the base of the skull, affecting the nerves and causing irritation and pain. These postural shifts also produce uneven weight on lower backs, which in turn cause painful muscle spasms and inflammatory pain. Instead of having the postural distortions realigned, correcting the primary cause of the pain, many people will reach for a pill or a prescription drug to help them alleviate the pain. These medications will do nothing for realigning the body structure, restoring the restricted areas back to normal or correcting spinal subluxations, which are misalignments of the vertebrae of the spinal cord that cause irritation and imbalance of the nervous system.

Many times during an examination of a patient I will find these musculoskeletal problems that cause imbalance to the nervous system to be the primary diagnosis. The spine often becomes twisted just like wringing out a dishrag. This causes compression of the nerves and vertebrae, which then results in pain. People who suffer from chronic muscle pain, muscle weakness, chronic headaches, back and neck pain and other musculoskeletal complaints usually have a problem of nerve irritation. Many times you see it in the elderly, whose bodies are bent forward so far that they are looking at the ground when standing erect. Sometimes people cannot turn their head to one side, having to turn their whole bodies around when backing their car out of the driveway. Usually with only a few simple adjustments of the spinal column and other restricted areas, these problems can be eliminated.

The entire body's function is driven by the nerve impulses that are generated through the nervous system. The body requires movement in order to generate much of the nerve energy required to keep the cells alive and healthy. This in turn stimulates the anatomy of the brain, causing the corresponding brain part to stay active and healthy. When any of the moveable structures of the body (for example, spine, rib cage, arms and legs) become restricted in their movement, the nerve centers from that area begin to decrease in function. This in turn produces weakness of the surrounding areas as well as a decrease in the stimulation that is required for the needs of the nervous system and brain.

When the nerve impulses decline, the nerves in that area and other functionally related areas (organs or other body parts that work synergistically with the affected area) as well as the brain begin to atrophy (deteriorate). The only way to restore these areas back to health is through realignment, which restores motion back to the restricted areas. This realigning process can happen through exercise, stretching and chiropractic adjustments. In doing so, the motion restores, the nervous system begins to function properly, and the body immediately begins to heal itself; that is the way we were designed.

I cannot tell you how many times I have relieved biomechanical stress with only one adjustment, and the relief is so dramatic that the patient thinks I have performed a miracle. Sometimes they can raise their arms over their head for the first time in years or perhaps squat down without pain when previously they could not even bend their knees. Often people are assisted or carried into my clinic because of intense pain, and after a simple adjustment, they practically dance out of the office. Many times people have come to my clinic with paralyzed limbs, impaired hearing or eyesight and a wide variety of chronic sicknesses and debilitating disorders. They have been restored to health simply by removing the nerve interference involved in their condition.

The Nervous System

I personally feel that most sicknesses and diseases in the body are caused from imbalances and disruptions in the communication between the brain and the nervous system, caused by trauma, deficiency, toxicity, infection and stress. The automatic or autonomic nervous system (ANS) continually monitors these conditions and "automatically" responds to changes in the body and nervous system in an effort to restore balance. The ANS consists of motor nerves to smooth muscle, cardiac muscle, adrenal glands and glands such as salivary, gastric and sweat glands.

There are two divisions of the ANS—the sympathetic and the parasympathetic. An oversimplified definition of their function is as follows:

- The sympathetic division provokes the fight-or-flight response, basically speeding you up when necessary to meet the demands of stress.

- The parasympathetic division dominates during non-stressful situations, such as aiding normal digestion and slowing the heart to normal.

These are their main priorities, though their design is much more intricate and complicated than we can explain here. It will help just to understand that the sympathetic speeds you up and the parasympathetic slows you down. The two systems are working hand in hand speeding up and slowing down organs, muscles, glands and other body systems to maintain the balance that is required to meet the body's constant demands. If a factor in life causes an imbalance by stimulating or suppressing either one of these nervous systems, the body will respond by displaying symptoms of illness.

For example, if the adrenal glands are stimulated, they respond by secreting hormones. This hormone production causes the sympathetic nervous system to produce a fight-or-flight response that affects the entire body. The heart beats faster with harder contractions, the breathing rate increases, pupils dilate and blood pressure may rise as well. In other words, the body *speeds up*. There are a variety of factors that can provoke this response: food, stress from chemicals, electromagnetic fields (such as radio and x-ray), biomechanical restrictions, extreme heat or cold as well as emotional, physical or environmental factors. Any of these factors, either by themselves or in combination, can negatively affect this entire autonomic balance.

Although conventional medical science does address many of these factors, sadly, the end result of their proposed treatment remains the same: drugs or surgery. As I have stated, there are times when these interventions and procedures are necessary. But it is my conviction that we need to take a more whole body—whole person—approach, based on the patient's individual needs. As physicians, we should do thorough examinations and make recommendations that address needs for the entire body, not just the obvious symptoms.

For example, patients have come to my clinic with headaches, and we discover the primary cause to be a food allergy. Other patients come with headaches, and my examination shows the cause to be a biomechanical restriction in the lower spine, which is causing stimulation to the sympathetic nervous system as well as bombarding the cerebellum with impulses, causing imbalance and producing a headache. In one case, the remedy was to remove a food from the diet; in the other, it required an adjustment to the lower back to restore the range of motion. Because headaches can be caused from anything ranging from hormone imbalance to brain tumors, I am not a big fan of just taking an over-the-counter prescription medication to cover up the pain.

We need to understand clearly that symptoms are warning signs from the body. They should not be brushed aside or suppressed with medication simply to keep someone happy or comfortable. I entirely approve of assisting the alleviation of pain and inflammation with medications that control symptoms as long as the primary cause for the distress is being addressed and treated. It is important not to ignore symptoms, as some do, for years before having them evaluated by healthcare professionals or even trying to research the problem on their own.

You May Need to See a Doctor

The five most dangerous words that a patient can ever say are: *Maybe it will go away!* Many times a diagnosis requires not only a description of symptoms, but also proper history, examination and test results that should complete a picture for the physician to help establish the underlying cause of the patient's problem. If you have attempted to correct your problems by yourself, even following the recommendations in this book, and are still experiencing uncomfortable symptoms, please let a physician evaluate your condition. If a symptom persists, it means something is going on in your body that is unrecognized and needs to be fixed.

Here are my recommendations for choosing the right physician for the problem you are having. Of course, my first rule is to ask the doctor if he or she is a Christian. After you are satisfied with that answer, I recommend that you see a qualified doctor according to the following criteria:

CHOOSING A PHYSICIAN

Type of Physician	Treatment for
Medical Doctors (M.D.) or Osteopathic Physicians (D.O.)	Emergency medicine (acute care, stabilization care, surgery, physical therapy, rehabilitation)
Chiropractic Doctor (D.C.)	Biomechanical and structural problems: spinal, joints, muscle spasm, nervous system imbalances (pain, numbness, tingling, burning), nutrition and diet; source of alternative medicines

Naturopathic Doctor (N.D.)	Herbal and nutrient therapies: alternative treatments, colonic irrigations, herbal detox and internal cleansing
Homeopathic Doctor (D.H.M.)	Chronic disorders, detoxification, supports all other therapies listed above, no known side effects

Note: Many physicians have taken postgraduate courses and are certified to practice treatments from several of the therapies listed above.

As a chiropractic physician, it is my greatest joy to remove pain and sickness permanently for my patients. Recently a patient who was in excruciating pain came to see me. He walked very slowly, wincing with every movement because of the pain. During his first treatment, some minor realignments were established, and he immediately began jumping up and down, cheering and praising God because he was so excited to be free from his prison of pain. Another patient arrived with a one-sided paralysis from suffering a stroke. He had lost the entire function of his left foot. After thirty minutes of treatment, the foot began to work as before his stroke. We cried together from the joy we shared in that healing experience. I am privileged to help people like these two patients every day with similar results.

The term *chiropractic* literally translated means "practice of the hands." As a practicing chiropractor, I like to consider the biblical promise that says, "They shall lay hands on the sick, and they shall recover" (Mark 16:18), as a special message to me and my like-minded colleagues. Perhaps the context of the verse refers to touching a person and praying for him, as we have been taught. But as I lay hands on a person to help to determine the primary cause of his problem and realign his physical structure, I very often whisper a prayer and expect God to guide my hands and help me to correct the problem so the body can heal.

In graduate school for chiropractic medicine, I learned two very important concepts that are vital to becoming a successful physician. These concepts have a biblical basis, as you will easily recognize:

- Healing first comes from above, then down, inside and out. God is the author, and man is the recipient as healing works first of all within and then manifests outwardly.

- Live with lasting purpose: Give for the sake of giving, love for the sake of loving and serve for the sake of serving.

I challenged you in the beginning to read these pages with an open mind and allow your belief system to be challenged. May I suggest that the next time you find yourself dealing with pain, suffering or an unsolved health problem, you consider a chiropractic physician? I am sure you will be pleasantly surprised with the results. If someone you know had a bad experience with a chiropractor, it is most likely the problem of that particular practitioner; that does not make the healing philosophy of chiropractic medicine less powerful. Find a chiropractic physician with whom you feel comfortable and who provides you with good results.

You may ask, "What kind of training do they receive?" Chiropractors are the only holistic practitioners who are national board certified in addition to being licensed by state boards in all fifty states. To compare the current curriculum structure for a doctor of chiropractic medicine with that of a medical physician, please see Appendix B.

The next time you are suffering symptoms of sickness, remember to seek the primary cause for the symptoms instead of just looking for relief by treating symptoms. If your physician does not give you a primary cause for your illness, try chiropractic. It is the best-kept secret of highly skilled healthcare that is based on finding the primary cause to bring about true healing, which then brings long-term health benefits.

A Society of Carboholics

Where did you learn how to obey God and to walk in understanding of His requirements for your life? More than likely, you have read the Word of God, attended church and listened to gifted ministers teach the Word of God. It is likely that you have read other books that taught godly principles as well. You have allowed the Spirit of truth, which is the Holy Spirit, to guide you and be your Counselor. If you have learned to obey the Word of God in these ways, you are undoubtedly living a fruitful and productive spiritual life.

Now, think for a moment to determine where you learned most of your knowledge regarding how to care for your body, your nutritional requirements and other lifestyle factors that impact your health. Chances are your response would involve gathering news from different forms of media regarding scientific studies, analytical data, statistics and blatant advertisements to sell a product that is deemed "healthy." Perhaps your doctor has given you some advice based on his medical studies and current theories of health. The point is, you probably have not received much understanding of how God designed you to live for health: what to eat, what to avoid and how to apply biblical principles to your body's well-being.

As I have stated, there are many sick Christians in spite of the fact that we are promised healing through the Atonement of Christ. What is the missing link? Why do I see so many sick Christians in my clinic? Statistics say that the leading cause of death in America last year was heart disease, the second leading cause was cancer, and the third cause was stroke.[1] According to statistics from the National Institutes of Health, seventeen million Americans had diabetes in 2000, with one million more cases being diagnosed each year in people twenty years of age and older.[2]

> THERE ARE MANY SICK CHRISTIANS IN SPITE OF THE FACT THAT WE ARE PROMISED HEALING THROUGH THE ATONEMENT OF CHRIST.

Unfortunately, many of the people who are part of these statistics are Christians. In my own clinical practice, using overall health as a measuring stick, there is not much difference between the number of "sick" non-Christians and the number of "sick" Christians I treat. Every year during the flu season as many Christians seem to be infected with the virus as nonbelievers. One of the main causes of these illnesses relates to the carboholic society that we have become.

What Is a Carboholic?

> A carboholic is a person whose body craves starchy or sugary foods. From time to time they find themselves eating too much for no good reason. No matter how much they want to control their eating, the urge for more overpowers them. At these times it is as if they can't keep from overeating.[3]

Carboholic tendencies may also be caused by an imbalance—an over-release of the hormone insulin when carbohydrate-rich foods are eaten.

As I studied the growing phenomenon of obesity, especially in the young, I began to understand that we are becoming a nation of addicts—not just to drugs and alcohol, but to food as well. Millions of people, including children, are addicted to food in the sense that it exerts inordinate power over them. They are governed by insatiable appetites, with cravings for foods that scarcely merit the name *food*…fast foods, they are called, which are filled with chemicals, sugar, salt and other damaging ingredients to health. Our children's bodies are being formed by these "nonfoods." And their appetites are ruled by the need for increasingly greater quantities of food.

While food is a gift of God, and the pleasure that accompanies eating is also His gift to us, I am reminded of the declaration that the apostle Paul made regarding all of God's gifts to us:

> All things are lawful unto me, but all things are not expedient: all things are lawful for me, but *I will not be brought under the power of any.*
> —1 Corinthians 6:12, emphasis added

The Cause of Food Addiction

Food, much of it the wrong kind, has gained an addictive power over many people without their even realizing it. They crave the sugary, spicy tastes that do not come with fresh vegetables and even nutritional fruits and whole grains. The nutrients their bodies—bones, nerves, brains and teeth—need are lacking in most of the foods they eat. They have become carboholics, eating mostly starchy and sugary "foods."

What contributes largely to this state is that most of the foods people are consuming are refined food products. *Refined* simply means a whole-food product that is broken down into foodstuff and separated from the life-giving nutrients that are subject to spoilage so that it will last longer on the shelf. The result is lifeless food, void of nutrients, which the body metabolizes and uses for fuel. The fact that these foods are altered (refined) results in their depleted nutrient quality. The refining process strips foods of many of the vitamins, minerals, essential fatty acids and other nutrients needed for proper maintenance of the body.

The body recognizes that it is not receiving the living nutrients it needs and responds to its need by sending hunger signals—cravings—which are usually answered by more of the same kind of lifeless foods. The end result is more people eating more food to try to satisfy their hunger. Restaurants have accommodated this scenario by offering "biggie" sizes that include double or triple burgers, upsized fries and giant soft drinks. It is sad to see the masses becoming massive, while their bodies are continually receiving less of the vital nutrients they need to keep them healthy. The truth is that people are eating ten dollars worth of food that is only giving them ten cents worth of nutrition.

Another vital concern is that the nutrients that are missing in these types of refined foods are the ones that help metabolize food, breaking it down into cellular energy (ATP). When the body can't break food down efficiently in order for it to become cellular building blocks, the body either eliminates the food or stores it as fat. The term *carboholic* has been coined for our society because the refined foods consumed are primarily carbohydrates. When a carbohydrate is refined (separated from its natural nutrient composition), the body metabolizes it into sugar immediately after the carbohydrate is consumed.

This rapid metabolic process, which is unhealthy, causes the pancreas to release a surge of insulin, a powerful hormone, in the body. Insulin in turn causes the body to store fat and elevate cholesterol. When individuals continue to bombard their system daily with refined carbohydrates, the body's fat storage dramatically increases, leading inevitably to weight gain. The fact that the body is being forced to use sugar for fuel, instead of fat, eventually damages the body's ability to break down fats properly. When that happens, the body stores extra proteins, carbohydrates and fats all as fats.

Most refined foods have a very bland taste because of loss of nutrient content, so many manufacturers add sugar to improve the taste. Foods that you may not suspect of having sugar content may show sugar as the second or third ingredient on the label, meaning it is the second or third largest ingredient. This extra sugar causes the pancreas to make a quick dump of insulin into the system, as we have stated, which then uses up the sugar very quickly, causing the body to crave more sugar.

This cycle causes an illness known as hypoglycemia. During a hypoglycemic episode, a person will feel very weak and will often experience brain fog, headaches, fatigue and acid reflux, to name a few symptoms. At times, they may even pass out. When people, especially women, continue these episodes untreated for years, their bodies deteriorate, eventually creating even worse health conditions such as diabetes.

A "Carboholic" Food Pyramid

Refined foods seem to be the primary food source of our fast-paced, suburban, microwave, working-mom society. Part of the reason we are eating this way can also be attributed to the food pyramid recommended by the government. It encourages people, who may consult it sincerely, wanting to eat well, to eat from six to eleven servings of cereals, grains, pasta, rice and bread. While this recommendation may not be a problem for a Mediterranean society, where these would be whole foods made from intact grains, it is problematic for our culture where refined foods reign.

Eating this quantity of refined carbohydrates daily, which metabolize straight to sugar, along with any added sugar products, will result in an overweight, overstressed society. When sugar is a main food consumed, in its myriad of forms of refined foods, the body literally becomes addicted to it; it acts like a drug. The body then craves its "drug" fix to make up for the energy losses caused by the lack of nutrients in the food it is given. The short-term bursts of energy that sugar provides need to be replenished quickly by more sugar intake in order to continue to satisfy the body's cravings. Much like a drug addict, people will continually turn to soft drinks, candy bars and other forms of sugary, refined food products in order to satisfy their cravings. Unfortunately, addicts crave the very thing that's killing them. What the food pyramid has successfully done is create a generation of carboholics.

It has also contributed largely to the obesity of our population. You may be aware that farmers who want to fatten up their livestock before they are slaughtered feed them grains. Grains are the surest way to increase their body fat to bring a better price.

Common sense will tell you that our food pyramid contributes to obesity by recommending that we eat so many servings of food based in grains, especially refined products.

Creating a Metabolic Imbalance

The government recommendation for eating quantities of carbohydrates (which we purchase mostly in their refined form) causes significant inability of the body to balance its blood sugar. Whole foods would not cause this imbalance, because they contain a balance of nutrients within themselves. For example, a sugar beet in its natural form has all of the vitamins, minerals, carbohydrates, proteins and minimal fat content to help balance the spoonful or so of sugar that it contains. So when you eat a sugar beet, it helps the body digest it without creating an imbalance of sugar.

The problem begins when the sugar beet is refined, losing its other nutrients that help it create balance; when it is introduced into the digestive system, there are no nutrients to offset or balance the effects of the sugar. Now the sugar is in a concentrated form, which will have a spiking effect on insulin and other metabolic processes in the body. The effect is much the same as if you ate orange juice concentrate by the spoonful. This scenario is true of most refined foods.

God is the perfect chemist; the whole foods He created are balanced nutritionally to support their proper utilization as they travel through the digestive system. We get into trouble when these whole foods are refined so that they are depleted of the vital nutrients needed to help them metabolize efficiently. That is why it is so important today to find ways, largely through supplementation, to add back into our diets the vitamins, minerals, essential fatty acids, amino acids, enzymes and coenzymes that are lacking from most of our foods.

Many people ride a hypoglycemic roller coaster for years because this severe disruption in the metabolic system affects many hormone systems. For example, the adrenal glands are definitely affected by surges of insulin in the system. The thyroid gland along with estrogen, testosterone and progesterone hormones are at risk for imbalance and compromise as a result of destructive eating habits.

New research suggests that a diet higher in protein and lower in carbohydrates than currently recommended may help people maintain desirable body weight and overall health.

> "For thirty years fad diets and various nutritional recommendations have come and gone," said Donald Layman, a professor of nutritional sciences at the University of Illinois. The result: Americans take in more calories than ever, obesity is at an all-time high and heart disease rates equal those of the 1970s.[4]

Carboholics are easy to pick out in a crowd. Most of them have dark circles under their eyes and a fatigued or "wiped out" look. They are usually overweight and have more rounded looking features. Many may have tried a variety of diets, which gives them a rapid weight loss initially, but then stalls as they reach a plateau. When they come off the diet, they usually gain all of the weight back that they had previously lost as well as an additional five to ten pounds. The reason they fail to maintain weight loss is that they are not beating their addiction.

WE ARE ADJUSTING OUR MENTALITIES TO ACCEPT OBESITY AS NORMAL.

When people try to clean up their diets, eating less sugary foods and refined carbohydrates, that is an improvement, but it is not the answer. If a person smokes five packs of cigarettes a day, for example, we consider that person to be addicted to nicotine. If he or she cuts the smoking down to five cigarettes a day, that is definitely a healthy improvement, but the fact that he still needs cigarettes shows he is still addicted. The only way to beat an addiction is to abstain from the addictive substance completely. Sugar addictions are no exception.

Our carboholic society has accepted as the "norm" the unhealthy diet represented by fast foods and refined carbohydrates. We are adjusting our mentalities to accept obesity as normal as well, which is a fatal deception. We need to consider what causes the demise of most Americans and what we can do personally to avoid becoming another "statistic."

Obese Children

An entire generation is being impacted by the carboholic culture we have created.

> Obesity in children has tripled in the past twenty years. A staggering 50 percent of adolescents in some minority populations are overweight. There is an epidemic of type 2 (formerly "adult onset") diabetes in children, and heart attacks may become a disease of young adults.[5]

Why is the health of our children deteriorating on such a scale? In 1995 the American Academy of Pediatrics stated that advertising to young children is inherently deceptive and exploitative. Yet each year the food industry spends an estimated $10 billion to influence the eating behavior of children. The average child sees ten thousand food advertisements per year, 95 percent of them for fast food, soft drinks, candy and sugared cereals—all high-profit and nutrition-poor products.[6]

I can't help wondering how the media would respond if obesity were any other illness that was impacting the health of an entire generation so drastically. I think it would be posted on the front page of every newspaper and given headlines in every news broadcast across the country. Is it possible that advertising promoting obesity with its junk foods pays the bills of the media, which is more important than our national health concerns? Or do we just think that the new size body is OK? People seem to be happy and adjusted to their larger size, and some show no concern for the health risk those extra pounds present.

For many of our children the average breakfast consists of a toaster pastry and a glass of milk. You may think that sounds pretty harmless. However, milk allergies and sensitivities are highly prevalent in children, which many parents never figure out.

I watched a video presentation in graduate school of a kindergarten child who was sitting in class drawing a picture of a house. He was very docile and well behaved. The teacher gave him a glass of milk to drink, and fifteen minutes later he went crazy. It was like watching a Jekyll and Hyde movie. The child started scratching his crayons across the paper violently. His entire demeanor changed as he became highly irritated and hyperactive.

The current way of eating we have accepted for our children is extremely harmful to them. You cannot send your children to school after feeding them a toaster pastry (full of sugar, which is a drug stimulant like rocket fuel) and a glass of milk ("Hyde potion") and expect them to be calm and to function efficiently.

The term ADHD (attention deficit hyperactivity disorder) has become far too normal a household—or classroom—word. It is currently an epidemic among our children. Of course, the pharmaceutical companies are there to save the day with drugs like Ritalin, a prescription medication with a patent and a large profit built into the sale. What is wrong with this picture?

We send children to school full of "rocket fuel" and "Hyde potion" and then forbid the teacher to teach them Bible principles such as the Ten Commandments or the "Golden Rule." Neither children nor teachers are allowed to pray. Teachers cannot use any kind of corporal discipline (spanking) to correct a child's misbehavior. Come on! There is something "badly wrong" here that seems unreasonable to me. Does it to you?

Unfortunately, we have become a society at risk, forfeiting our long-term health for carboholic diets that are promoted by billions of dollars of media advertising. It is sad that the bottom line for our "health" choices has become the dollar, which creates wealth for those who are jeopardizing our health. As we look at the major killers of our culture, you may discover lifestyle issues that you need to change to avoid them.

CHAPTER 4

America's Worst Killer Diseases

In America last year, the leading cause of death was *heart disease*. The second leading cause of death was *cancer*. And the third leading cause of death was *stroke*. Besides these top three killer diseases running rampant in our nation, sixty million Americans currently have *diabetes*, which for some will cause their final demise.[1]

In spite of a system that is as technologically advanced as our medical system, these statistics, which are released by government agencies, are becoming worse each year. For example, considering the statistics for cancer, the World Health Organization recently reported that global cancer rates could rise by 50 percent, to fifteen million cases per year by 2020.[2]

The Problem of Fats

If technology is supposedly advancing our medical system, and as a nation we are perceived as improving our healthcare, why are these statistics going the wrong way? Did you know that those top four conditions all share one common root? All four diseases—heart disease, cancer, stroke and diabetes—involve the harmful accumulation of fats in your body.

Heart disease and fat

To understand how fats become a problem, even though they are the preferred fuel of the body, consider heart disease. When you take the wrong types of fat into the body, they accumulate in the tissues of the body instead of being used for energy. After circulating in the system, they are stored in the fatty tissues and in the blood vessels and arteries. If your body is burning sugar and storing fats, this also occurs.

When they clog the vessels, the condition is called *atherosclerosis*. When atherosclerosis sets in, blood can't flow through nice big openings; it has to push its way through smaller openings, which causes the heart to work harder. As you may know, the heart is a muscle. If it has to work harder, it soon tires, and over a period of time you literally wear that muscle out, which leads to *heart disease*.

Clogged blood vessels also cause blood pressure to increase. When the body is not burning fat properly, blood pressure increases. And cholesterol, which is a "fatty hormone," begins to elevate, as well as triglycerides, which are formed from stored carbohydrates. So, as doctors, when we look at blood work and see these elevations of blood pressure, cholesterol and triglycerides, we know these symptoms mean that your heart may be in trouble. Part of your diagnosis would be an increased risk for heart disease, America's number one killer!

Cancer and fat

You may have more understanding of how fat affects heart disease, but you may wonder what fat accumulations have to do with cancer. It is still a common perception that no one knows what causes cancer. However, that is a misperception to a large degree, for many products on the market actually have to be labeled with a warning that they may cause cancer.

For example, the men who fought in the Vietnam War were exposed to something called *agent orange,* a chemical that produced cancer in many who were exposed to it. Do you remember the little pink packets that we used to sweeten our drinks with? When those packets first came out, they actually had to write on the packet that it could cause cancer. It was a chemical that had a taste similar to the taste of sugar. Many products that are on our grocery's shelves, especially on the pesticide aisle, contain warnings that exposure to them may cause cancer. It is fairly simple to deduce from these and other examples that chemicals play a large role in the cause of cancer.

Then where does accumulated fat fit into this picture? When we are exposed to chemicals and they are not properly eliminated from the body, they are being stored in the accumulated fat of the body. So environmental hazards, in the form of chemicals that the body absorbs and stores in the extra fat, are a major risk factor in the cause of cancer.

Stroke and fat

How is stroke related to accumulated fat? Unfortunately, the rate of strokes is increasing along with these other killers, as I noted earlier in this chapter. One major source of stroke is a hardened particle of accumulated fat that dislodges, floats through the bloodstream and then lodges in a critical area that blocks off oxygen to the brain. That blockage causes tissue or brain cells to die, which often causes paralysis to the face, arm and one side of the body (stroke).

While this may seem too simple an explanation of what causes a devastating illness, it is a fact that keeping the body cleansed and burning the proper fuel will greatly lessen the risk of stroke. Proper exercise that allows the cells of the body to breathe fresh oxygen and aids the cleansing process as well can also lessen the risk of stroke.

Diabetes and fat

Diabetes is running rampant, as the statistics we cited suggest. If people are not yet diagnosed with diabetes, many have a precondition to the disease, which is called hypoglycemia. As we discussed, we have become a nation of carboholics, due in part to government recommendations of the food pyramid that educates the public concerning the proper way to eat in order to stay healthy. We noted the problem caused by eating several servings of refined carbohydrates a day, as the pyramid suggests.

In the case of diabetes, instead of the heart wearing out, the pancreas wears out from having to pump so much insulin into the system to accommodate the high-sugar diets as a result of our overload of refined carbohydrates. When it wears out to the point that it can no longer produce insulin, we call that condition *diabetes*. Doctors have to prescribe to diabetics the hormone insulin because the pancreas can no longer make it.

Billion-Dollar Disease Industries

Of course, when millions of people become severely ill, they need expert medical care. If you buy into the lifestyle of eating that is being promoted today, you have a good chance of becoming a statistic—falling prey to heart disease, cancer, stroke, diabetes or other equally serious diseases. Because so many people have already done so, each of these diseases has become billion dollar industries.

For patients with heart disease, heart surgeries are available along with rehabilitation and other support systems. For cancer patients, there are chemotherapy and huge medical institutions that are designated for cancer research, funded by millions of dollars. Stroke victims also need treatment and rehabilitation centers, and diabetics require insulin and other care.

While these treatment protocols are helpful in extending life for many, they cannot prevent the disease or reverse the damage that your lifestyle choices have caused. I believe the biblical warning that the apostle Paul gave applies to our life situations regarding maintaining our bodies: "Be not conformed to this world: but be ye transformed by the renewing of your mind" (Rom. 12:2).

I have often heard the saying, "To continue doing the same thing expecting a different result is a form of insanity." Let me encourage you to expect to make changes in your lifestyle if you want to see different results. If you continue doing exactly what you're doing regarding eating habits and other lifestyle choices that impact your health, your chances are very good that you will become a disease "statistic."

Precursor to Disease

Obesity is the result of our carboholic society that often produces the killer diseases we have discussed. The accumulation of fats in the different areas of the body as a result of being overweight is often the main precursor to serious health problems. I wish that people who struggle with obesity would be concerned about the serious health problems their being overweight can cause. Instead, they seem to be concerned about how they look or what other people think of them.

The weight-loss industry has flourished as a result of people wanting to lose excess pounds, while eating the way they have always eaten, spending billions of dollars on weight-loss programs. Even the pharmaceutical companies got into the act with prescription drugs like fen-phen and Redux that were supposed to help people lose weight. Unfortunately, these drugs were responsible for thousands of deaths from heart attacks and other ills and had to be taken off the market.

Herbal products were touted to be the answer to weight loss, helping to burn body fat in combination. It is true that these thermogenics actually work; they do produce an effect in the body that will cause the body to burn fat. But they are not without harmful side effects. Many of these weight-loss formulas contain caffeine and other ingredients that will create a "speed" effect on the body in addition to functioning as diuretics. Because we are made of approximately 60 percent water, when we begin to take one of these products, we can immediately lose five to ten pounds of water weight, which is a significant loss of fluid. If this loss of body fluids is not properly managed, it can cause some serious side effects in the body.

Anytime you speed up the finely tuned body system, you are increasing the demands on the heart; you also create a tendency toward elevating blood pressure. If these effects are not managed properly, you face some serious health risks. While these products produce "results" of weight loss, it does not mean they are healthy options. I personally don't support this type of weight loss because it usually does not give lasting results; it is only addressing a symptom rather than the cause of obesity.

The Root Cause of Obesity

Why do Americans accumulate so many fats in their systems, causing the epidemic of obesity? It is very simple! It is because the common American diet doesn't contain the nutrients that help the body to burn fat. This forces the body to store the fats in the tissues of the body because it does not have the nutrients needed to break them down into energy. Your body has to have amino acids, vitamin and mineral catalysts, cofactors and enzymes all working together in your system in order to get the fats out of storage and into the fuel tank of the cell, called the *mitochondria.*

The body is designed to burn fat for fuel. One of the ways we know this is true is that when the body retains extra carbohydrates, they are stored as fat. When there are extra proteins in the body, they are stored as fat. And when extra fats remain in the body, they are also stored as fat. The body recognizes fat as its primary fuel source.

To help me illustrate the fact that the body is designed to burn fat, I want you to imagine that I am holding a log in my right hand. We will call it the "fat log." I have another log in my left hand, which we will call a "carbohydrate log." If I take the carbohydrate log and put it into the furnace of the cell (mitochondria), it will give me four kilocalories of energy per gram. If I take the fat log and throw it into the mitochondria, it will give me nine kilocalories of energy per gram. If you are concerned with having a higher energy level, which log would you rather burn for fuel? The obvious answer is the "fat log" because it will yield two and one-fourth times more energy per molecule than the carbohydrate log.

If you continually burn the carbohydrate log, you place your body in a state of "down-regulating," or giving it less energy than it needs to perform all of its functions. When you burn the fat log, you are "up-regulating" your body, making it more efficient in its activities. Let me explain.

How would you (and people you know) like to have two and one-fourth times your present energy levels? This higher energy level can be accomplished without harmful stimulation or speeding up of the metabolism. Simply by allowing the body to metabolize the fuel that produces more energy, you can return to the normal way the body was designed to function. It is this natural approach to burning fat that produces the best and most lasting weight loss.

Down-regulating

You may have *down-regulated* your system without even realizing it. When you eat sugary foods and carbohydrates, you soon become addicted to them, as we have mentioned, and become a carboholic. You are supposed to be in a "fat-burning" cycle, but instead, you get stuck in the "sugar-burning" cycle, which results in a much lower level of energy. You are burning the "carbohydrate log" instead of the "fat log."

Regardless of the fuel you are giving your body, your body functions require the same amount of energy to make the heart beat, the eyes blink, the lungs work and every other function you require of it. The energy resources needed for those vital functions will be used first, making all other energy needs expendable. When the body runs out of energy from the fuel it was given, it begins down-regulating in other areas.

For example, one of the major areas that your body down-regulates is your immune system. We call that being tired and run down or having low resistance. The result of having an immune system that has been down-regulated is that you get sick easier. You seem to be more susceptible to catching things such as cold and flu viruses that go around each year.

Up-regulating

Let's imagine that you begin to burn "fat logs" instead of "carbohydrate logs" to fuel the body. Because "fat logs" produce two and one-quarter times the energy of "carbohydrate logs," you would be able to up-regulate your system. One of the first results would be a strengthening of your immune system, which means you will be at much less risk for suffering all of the pathogens that go around each year. By avoiding sugary foods and consuming the right kinds of fats, you will start converting all of the stored fats in your body, using them for energy instead of allowing them to accumulate in the blood vessels or around the liver.

Another positive result of up-regulating your system would be helping the gallbladder. The gallbladder is designed to concentrate the bile from the liver so it can better break down fats for the body to use as fuel. When it does not receive the nutrients it needs, the bile is too weak to do its job, allowing the gallbladder to become filled with sludge that turns into stones. For this reason many people are having their gallbladders removed by surgery. The answer is to give the body the proper nutrients that will strengthen the bile so that it can break down the fats to be used for fuel. (See product page for *Daytime and Nighttime Take It Off* formulas.)

Hormone imbalance is another common complaint that I diagnose in my patients on a regular basis. (See chapter 7 for more discussion.) Let me explain simply the breakdown of hormones in the body. Cholesterol is the fatty hormone that converts to pregnenolone; pregnenolone converts to DHEA; DHEA converts into testosterone, estrogen and progesterone. If your body is breaking down cholesterol properly, it allows the body to produce the proper balance of sex hormones.

Men who suffer from low testosterone levels have no sex drive, and women who suffer with hot flashes, menstrual cramps and other difficulties are showing signs that their bodies are not properly regulated. If we can get the body to burn fat, it will metabolize cholesterol and then proceed to balance the hormones itself. This is a better solution than giving synthetic hormones (which have side effects and cause other problems) or putting chemical drugs in the body (which bombard the liver). When liver function is decreased, the toxic chemicals you are getting from your environment begin to back up in your system, causing cancer and other diseases.

Let me encourage you to go for the cause of the problem! Get "fat logs" out of storage in the tissues of your body and into the fuel tank, the mitochondria, of the cell. Your energy level will automatically rise, and you will up-regulate your whole system. That means you will strengthen every function of your body, which will then be able to resist disease.

When you understand how incredibly complex the body's functions are in its quest for health, you should want to make lifestyle choices that are healthy for your body. It is important to get your system cleansed of these fatty deposits, turning them into energy so that you feel better and your body works better. Proper nutrition will go a long way to accomplishing this task.

Helpful protocols

I formulated a supplement combination called *Take It Off—Daytime,* which is filled with amino acids and vitamin/mineral catalysts as well as other enzymes and cofactors necessary to assist your body in breaking down fats. When you get these nutrients into the system, the body will be able to fix the fat accumulation problem. These nutrients actually help the body move the fat into the furnace to use for fuel. If you take this product twenty minutes before lunch, the nutrients are all ready to help metabolize the food when you eat it. (Please see product page for ordering information.)

Another product I formulated, *Take It Off—Nighttime,* can be taken at night on an empty stomach, at least three hours before you go to bed. During the night it helps the body put accumulated fats into the fuel tank, helping your body to up-regulate itself all night. This results in having extra energy built up for when you awaken, to help you to get your day started full of energy. These supplements help the body to heal, giving it more energy to repair the damage it sustains from the wide variety of environmental stresses it will face.

It is also important to understand that there is a lot of garbage in the stored fat in your body. You may be aware that your body has filters that help to cleanse your system of toxic wastes. For example, your liver is your "*chemical* filter," your kidneys are your "*fluid* filters," and your spleen is your "*blood cell* filter." Your lymphatic system is your "*intercellular* filter system," and your lungs and their airways are your "*air* filters." Of course, your colon is the "*catch-all* filter"—it filters all the waste of the other filters. You need to make sure your filters are all cleansed regularly.

God made natural foods and herbs of the field to cleanse these filters safely and effectively without side effects. For example, if I say, "Prunes and oatmeal," what do you think? That's right—colon cleansing. There are a host of herbs that cleanse the colon safely and effectively—alfalfa, psyllium and fibers, to name a few. And there is a classification of herbs that are called bitters; when you put them on your tongue, they taste bitter. These herbs do a good job of cleansing the liver and the gallbladder. Certain grasses are very good for cleansing the kidneys. Each "filter" in your body has a designated set of herbs that cleanse it very well and do so naturally without side effects.

I formulated a product called *Tea Tox*, which is a combination of herbal cleansers that you can take every night before you go to bed. While you are sleeping, these herbs work to clean your filters, flushing harmful chemicals out of the body so that your system can begin to up-regulate itself into greater health.

After cleansing your system, you might want to try a product I formulated called *Life Support,* which contains vitamins, minerals, nutrients, essential fatty acids and enzymes, many of which are missing in our diets. Replacing them in your system will help to stop cravings for foods that do not nourish the body. (See product page for ordering information.)

However you choose to supplement your nutrition in order to give your body what it needs to function in health, you will also need to eliminate harmful "foodstuffs" to which you may be addicted. Take inventory of what kinds of foods you most often eat, what you have in your refrigerator and on your shelves. Begin to eat more fresh foods that have not been refined and have no chemicals added, and you will see a difference in your energy levels. If you want to find whole, healthy foods, shop the aisles around the outside perimeters of your grocery store. You'll find less advertising and more nutritional benefits than in the center aisles.

Periodic Evaluation

It is very important that everyone evaluate his or her health periodically. Health is like the proverbial camel of which it is said, "The last straw broke its back." You can keep putting straws (stresses) on your health until one small incident causes it to collapse. There are four main causes of stress to the body:

1. Nutrient deficiency: Deficiency can be caused from lack of nutrients or the body's inability to break down, absorb and utilize nutrients.

2. Toxicity: A toxic condition can be caused from over-exposure to toxic buildup or by the body's lack of ability to excrete toxins. Three main groups of toxins are chemicals, heavy metals and food sensitivities.

3. Infection: Microorganisms are opportunists that lie dormant waiting for their opportunity to attach when the body's resistance is lowered. If a person's immune system is chronically lowered, these infectious microorganisms gain momentum, creating a constant drain on the body's energy levels. Three main groups of infectious organisms are yeast, parasites and viruses.

4. Metabolism: Metabolic issues are primarily caused from the wrong type of energy conversion, from hormone imbalances or glandular dysfunction. The two main causes of faulty energy conversion are the carboholic syndrome (burning sugar) and events that suppress the thyroid.

The body is continually monitoring these four potential problems—deficiency, toxicity, infections and metabolism—as it attempts to resist disease and maintain proper function. If subgroups in these four categories become unbalanced or accentuated, the entire system can be affected, resulting in symptoms, sickness and disease. I have developed a health survey, which you can find on page 161, that you can take to determine which areas of your health are giving you a problem. Each section on the health survey represents one of these four areas: Category A represents deficiency, category B represents toxicity, category C represents infections, and category D represents metabolism. I encourage you to take time to respond to the survey to determine your present health needs.

When you take responsibility for your health, you don't have to live in fear, worrying about whether or not you will become a statistic of one of America's killers. Your body is well equipped to handle whatever it needs to resist; it just needs the proper kinds and amount of nutrients (fertilizer), the flushing of its filters (herbal preparations and exercise) and plenty of good clean water. When you provide your body with what it needs, your body knows how to do the rest all by itself.

In the next chapters, we will explore in more detail how you can build your body's health by learning to care for it as the Creator's gift to you.

SECTION II

PROMOTING CELLULAR HEALTH

Leave your drugs in the chemist pot if you can heal the patient with food.

—HIPPOCRATES, THE FATHER OF MEDICINE

CHAPTER 5

Feed
the Cell

Why do you eat? Because you get hungry? To satisfy your cravings? To enjoy a pleasant pastime? I'm sure that eating your favorite foods makes you happy, but do you know why you were you *designed* to eat? From birth, eating is a vital, time-consuming part of our lives. Children are coached and cajoled by adults to "clean your plate" and "eat your veggies." And we quickly learn the things we love to eat and beg to have more of them. Eating is so natural and fills so much time each day that we rarely think about why we do it; we just do it.

Eating is much more than an enjoyable pastime or a way to satisfy our hunger. Eating is God's design to continually replenish the body with fuel for renewed energy and to maintain health. Isn't it wonderful that God also made eating enjoyable? And aren't you glad that you don't have to be concerned with how the food you eat is digested in your body? You just eat it, and the body knows what to do with it to turn it into energy.

However, if you need to find answers for health problems, or if you simply want to maintain health and avoid problems, it will be helpful to understand a little about how your body handles the food you give it. Let's explore a little biochemistry to understand what's happening in your body, without your ever knowing it, every time you eat.

Maintaining the Design

If you are a typical American living in the fast lane, you just grab whatever you can for lunch, shove it into your mouth, move your teeth around a few times and swallow it half chewed. Then you guzzle down some type of liquid that may contain as much as 9 or 10 teaspoons of sugar to rinse your mouth. However, your body is ready, from the first half-chewed mouthful, to begin its complex action of digesting the food you give it, attempting to satisfy all the functions of the body and use it as fuel for energy.

Your body knows that it must break down any food you feed it into three main categories: proteins, carbohydrates and fats. It begins to convert the enzymes it needs to do that complicated digestive process, which begins in your mouth. After your body's enzymes begin the digestive process, breaking down the proteins, carbohydrates and fats, your food must still be broken down into smaller molecules. The protein, carbohydrate and fat molecules are too big for the cell to be able to metabolize. They must be metabolized further to provide food for the cells.

Making "cell food"

The body then releases other catalysts and chemicals to further break down:

- *Proteins* into amino acids

- *Fats* into essential fatty acids

- *Carbohydrates* into basic sugars

Even after this complex digestive process, the food you ate is not digested into small enough units for the cells to use for fuel and energy. The tiny molecules that have been formed have to travel down *conjugation pathways*, in which proteins go through a process called *transamination*, carbohydrates go through *glucuronidation* and fats go through *beta-oxidation*. These metabolic pathways cause the food molecules to break down into a still smaller molecule called the *pyruvate*, which is still not acceptable as food for the cell. One vital element is lacking.

Oxygen: a vital element

Even when the body has done the work to provide the cell with food, one more element is required to transform the tiny pyruvate molecule into actual cell food, or acetyl-CoA. That element is *oxygen*. Even though oxygen is plentiful in the air around us, many people do not have the needed oxygen activated in their bodies to aid digestion, the feeding of the cells.

Our sedentary lifestyles do not involve us in necessary *aerobic* activity, which literally means "in the presence of oxygen," to supply our cells with the oxygen they require for health. Without proper exercise, which would circulate oxygen throughout the one hundred trillion cells of the body, there is not enough oxygen present to convert the food into cell food. When this happens, even though you may be eating ten dollars worth of food, your body will be able to convert only about ten cents worth of nutrition to feed your cells.

Assuming that you get enough exercise to bring oxygen into the system, your body will then break your lunch into the final form of nutrient, which enables the cell to "eat" it. Those nutrients will in turn be converted into cellular energy, called ATP energy, to be used by the body for its many activities.

For those who don't exercise enough to get the needed oxygen into the cells, the pyruvate cannot be transformed into energy, and instead, it converts into lactic acid. Lactic acid is what makes muscles sore when you are overactive. For example, maybe you have worked out with weights or played the "weekend warrior," and when you tried to get out of bed the next morning you looked like the tin man, walking stiffly and needing help to put on your socks. Lactic acid buildup can develop into all kinds of mysterious pain cycles (arachidonic acid, leukotriene production and so forth).

What do you do when you experience this kind of muscle pain? You may be in the habit of taking an aspirin, ibuprofen or acetaminophen to get instant relief. Although these pills do make you feel better for a while, they also cause liver and kidney stress, killing some vital cells in your body, which will eventually cause more serious problems.

My suggestion for sore muscles and stiffness is to get up and move around a little bit, go out and start walking around slowly, until you can build up to maybe a little faster pace. Keep moving until you can get the heart rate up to about 130 to 150 beats per minute so you get some good circulation of the oxygen and get good aerobic—in the presence of oxygen—activity. That will aid the body's digestion, so that when the pyruvate molecules are formed, there will be enough oxygen in your system to convert those molecules into cell food instead of lactic acid. Proper, ongoing exercise will assist the body in digesting food, making it provide energy instead of pain.

Choose Lasting Results

Of course, this method for relieving pain requires some effort and time investment. And the pharmaceutical companies would rather not promote exercise because it is free! You won't need to buy their pain-killing pills if you are making lifestyle choices that get rid of your pain without cost. Their ads encourage you to live any way you want, and then when your body protests, they will be there for you—delivering pain relief for a profit. And they deliver what they promise—relief that lasts several hours. After that, the pain is back, and you are looking for that bottle again. When you continue to buy into that system, you become a lifetime customer, which makes for a lucrative business!

One study shows that people who take just one ibuprofen or acetaminophen (which is equivalent to a Tylenol or an Advil) per day for a year double their chances for end-stage kidney disease and/or renal failure. One thousand pills over a lifetime of consumption will produce the same results.[1] Somehow, the commercials leave these painful facts out. In my clinical practice, I have learned that for every "quick fix" there is a hook, which will bring negative consequences in time.

On the other hand, when we choose to live by godly principles, taking personal responsibility for our body, it takes time, diligence and consistency to bring lasting results. It is like planting seed to grow a harvest. If you stick a seed in the ground, it isn't going to pop up corn in one day. You have to tend it, giving it the nourishment it needs to grow. But if you nurture it carefully, eventually you will have a healthy plant. That kind of nurturing care is necessary as well to have a healthy, pain-free, drug-free body.

Unfortunately, when it comes to our health, we want it right now, instantly, after abusing our bodies for years and suffering the consequences of our lifestyle. People who have abused their bodies, requiring their systems to reproduce red blood cells without proper amounts of oxygen and to make brain cells out of hamburgers and french fries, cannot expect to function mentally at a superior level.

To maintain God's intricate design, as we have described it briefly, for the body to maintain and refuel itself in health, we must make wise choices regarding the food we give it. Shortly after He created mankind, God told Adam and Eve how to eat. God's Word instructs us that basically all the plants, both fruit and vegetable, are for our nourishment (Gen. 1:29). Later, He added the meats that were good for consumption as well (Gen. 9:3; 1 Tim. 4:3). While

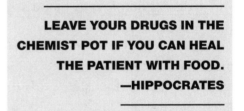

LEAVE YOUR DRUGS IN THE CHEMIST POT IF YOU CAN HEAL THE PATIENT WITH FOOD.
—HIPPOCRATES

we do not intend to discuss dietary laws here, we can understand God gave us basic principles that involve natural foods, which He designed for our health.

We have to eat the fruits, vegetables and plants because they draw nutrients out of the soil that our body has to have for digestion to take place and to give us life and energy. Plants take nutrients called minerals from the soil; from the sunlight they make vitamins. Other healthful chemical reactions take place through photosynthesis in their little stems and leaves. When you eat them, you begin to digest all of those nutrients, which your body has to have to function properly. Whether you like it or not, you were designed by the Creator to run on "high-octane" plant food. While we are certainly not suggesting a totally vegetarian diet, we are explaining the body's need for these vital nutrients found only in plants.

Cure for Complicated Ills

I've heard people say, "Yeah, when people take vitamins, minerals and nutrients, that only benefits the companies that sell those products." I want to respond that the Word of God teaches us to care for the body, and giving the body the nutrients it needs is part of that care. It is an accepted fact that the food produced today does not contain all the nutrients we need; therefore, we need to supplement so that our bodies are not deprived of the nutrients they need. This is how we were designed to function. And if you do not get the nutrients you need, the symptoms will show up.

In other words, if you deprive your body of something it needs, it will create a symptom. Have you ever been hungry and heard your stomach start to growl? Then, if you don't eat, your knees may get weak. You may soon get a headache. Then your mood even changes; you get the grumps. Your blood sugar eventually drops to the point that you get mean.

I have been in a church service, preaching to people who were pleasant and enthusiastic; they would be laughing and singing hallelujah in the service. Afterwards they would greet me, smile, shake my hand and say, "Love you, Doc!"

Thirty minutes later, I would meet them again at a restaurant, and they would be screaming at their kids to shut up and telling their spouse to hurry in an unkind tone. What happened? How could they change so radically in such a brief period of time?

Then I began to wonder what would happen if you showed up at a doctor's office with the symptoms I just described. The doctor would probably begin to diagnose your symptoms upon examining them. He would hear the growling noises in your stomach and call it *borborygmus*. The next symptom to diagnose would be the weak knees, which he would call *malaise* and *fatigue*. You could then say you were diagnosed with borborygmus, malaise and fatigue. Those are good words. Then the doctor would probably refer to your headache as *cephalgia*. And if you told the doctor you were happy one minute and screaming the next, he might diagnose you as *bipolar*.

Most people seem to relish their diagnoses. Someone who is

diagnosed with these symptoms may be talking with his friend and say, "Yeah, mine is the worst case the doctor ever saw."

"Oh, really?" the friend responds. "What is it?"

"Borborygmus, fatigue, malaise and cephalgia."

Of course, the doctor will give you a medication for every one of those symptoms. You can try to fix those symptoms, but you are not fixing the cause of them. What do you suppose would fix the cause of that problem? EAT!

That is just too simple; it does not involve a scientific diagnosis. The skeptic responds, "Do you mean to tell me that if I give my body the nutrition it needs, all of these symptoms will go away?" Yes! Emphatically, *yes.*

Sometimes it is that simple to eliminate symptoms of illness. Perhaps that is why God said in His Word that He chose the foolish things of the world to confound the wise (1 Cor. 1:27). I was foolish enough to believe what He said, foolish enough to grasp the principles for health He has given us and apply them in my life. I understand that my body is designed to heal; God put that incredible ability for healing in my body.

If you are ready to enter into the covenant of healing and health God has provided, I encourage you to open your mind to a greater understanding of how your body works. As we discuss the body's ability to metabolize foods and heal itself, you will gain the understanding you need to improve your health. Even Hippocrates, considered the father of medicine, declared that you should "leave your drugs in the chemist pot if you can heal the patient with food."

The Body Can Heal Itself

The body has a wide variety of types of cells. There are tissue cells, skin cells, organ cells, nerve cells, brain cells and blood cells, to list some basic categories. Though these cells have different functions, they all require the same elements for health: oxygen, fuel and activation. We have discussed briefly how fuel is formed for the cell through digestion. The body depends on its finely tuned nervous system to activate the distribution of these nutrients so they can be dispatched to meet the specific needs of each kind of cell.

Though all cells require water, oxygen and glucose, different types of cells also require very specific and targeted nutrients in order to meet their individual needs. For example, cells of organs require specific nutrients that nerve cells do not. And some cells require more of certain nutrients than others. These nutrients are dispatched to their destination via the vascular system—blood vessels, capillaries and veins. It is the nervous system that controls all of these dispatches to make sure every cell receives what it needs.

In other words, if the nervous system is healthy, it receives signals from deprived parts of the body and dispatches through the vascular system the proper nutrients that are needed. We have described the basic elements into which our food is broken down as proteins, carbohydrates and fats. Generally speaking, proteins are used for *cellular repair* and *replication*. Carbohydrates are used for *cellular metabolism*. And fats, which form the layers of the cell wall, are used for *insulation* and *lubrication*. These macronutrients have many uses that are far more complex than will be discussed in this book. However, a general understanding of how they work in your system will be helpful as you choose natural ways to improve your health.

Understanding Proteins

Proteins are found in their highest quantity in meats, eggs and cheese. Although soy and other vegetables do contain significant amounts of protein, meats, eggs and cheese are generally recognized as the basic proteins. The body breaks down protein by using proteolytic enzymes, which degrade the proteins into smaller amino acids, as we have mentioned.

Amino acids are nutrients that assist in healing and repairing the body in specific areas. Some amino acids such as L-carnitine and L-taurine, for example, are targeted to the heart. Others, such as leucine, isoleucine and valine, are targeted toward the large skeletal muscle groups. Once the proper amino acids reach their destinations, they initiate the healing, building and repairing process specific to their functions. This is occurring continually all day, every day in the human body, assuming that the body has the nutrients needed to form amino acids.

If the body becomes deficient, it will soon begin to break down. Even in its deteriorating state, the body knows to spare the most vital areas, feeding them by robbing other areas of the body. For example, during starvation, the body will rob proteins from muscles and tissues to send them to more vital areas where they are needed to maintain survival. Though this is an extreme example, it illustrates the mechanism that is functioning in every person.

When people choose to eat protein-deficient junk foods (processed and refined), they cause a depletion of protein throughout their system. Though they have enough food to remedy their hunger, that food does not nourish the body's health, so the body begins to break down. For this reason, when people visit my clinic for pain syndromes and degenerative types of disorders, my first recommendation is that they immediately eliminate junk food (fast foods, sweets, chips, crackers, sodas and so on).

Building blocks

Proteins are often called the building blocks of the body. Let me explain why that is true. In nerve cells (neurons), certain proteins are stimulated when muscles and joints move and stretch. For example, if someone exercises by using or stretching a muscle, it increases the nerve stimulation that activates certain genetic proteins, ultimately changing the actual DNA expression of those same cells. This in turn causes the cellular DNA to replicate to produce better and stronger nerve pathways that ultimately create a healthier, more stable nervous system. In this way, protein not only helps rebuild muscle tissues, but it also promotes a healthier communication throughout the body via the nervous system.

In today's world, proteins from red meats and animal products have become a concern. There seems to be a consensus that these proteins contribute to our top three killers—heart disease, cancer and stroke. However, civilizations have survived for thousands of years without these diseases wreaking havoc with their population.

I personally believe that eating red meat is not the basic problem causing these diseases.

Other factors involved that make red meat hazardous to health are a lack of exercise and overconsumption of sugars, including refined carbohydrates. The meats do not pose the problem for the body; it is sugar mixed with meat that creates the health problem, along with a sedentary lifestyle that does not produce enough oxygen for the body to metabolize proteins properly. Avoiding sugar and undergoing regular physical exercise will allow the body to break down easily the meats for protein utilization. The problem arises when people consume large amounts of meat (fuel) with little or no exercise (activation).

When the nervous system is activated by exercise, it increases its frequency of firing, which in turn helps improve elimination and digestive functions. Oxygen is supplied from aerobic types of exercise, which is required in order to break down protein to make ATP (energy). When a person exercises by walking, he increases the movement of waste material through the bowel, providing for a more optimal elimination of toxins as well. The amount of fat burned during exercise is stored as extra energy, which can later be used for digestion, healing and repair or a host of other vital functions.

Balancing protein

One problem with protein consumption is the quantity that is consumed at one time. When consuming proteins, a good rule to follow is to measure a *hand-size portion* of meat, eggs or cheese. Do not eat more than the quantity you can fit into the palm of your hand, measuring from where the wrist meets your hand to where the fingers join your hand. A person's own hand should be the measuring stick. It is all right to eat one hand-size portion of meat, eggs or cheese with each meal.

You have heard stories of farmers who have consumed large amounts of beef, ham, eggs and cheese, and yet live in health to a ripe old age. The secret to their health is they learned to get rid of the extra protein and fat through hard physical work, and it was utilized to repair their bodies. The key: *plenty of fuel and plenty of activation.* Unfortunately, the average person eats entirely too much *fuel* compared to the ratio of *activation.* Be honest with yourself and ask yourself this question: Do I need to decrease the amount of fuel (food), increase the activation (exercise) or both?

More active people may need to consume more proteins, perhaps choosing a good protein powder drink between meals. People who are more sedentary and do much less physical exercise need less protein, perhaps choosing to eat it with one or two meals daily. The balance of the meals between proteins, carbohydrates and fats should not change. If more protein is needed, it is better to add the extra protein at other times during the day.

Protein is your friend if eaten in the proper quantity and balance with other necessary foods. It can produce some unhealthy side effects if too large amounts are eaten. Problems can arise, as well, if you do not eat enough protein. Many people, especially those involved in weightlifting, consume entirely too many proteins. They may read about a diet that their favorite world champion power lifter has followed, and they try to do what that power lifter did. The problem is that because they are not world power lifters themselves, their dietary needs are not the same. Excess protein can cause the body to become acidic in nature. Many degenerative diseases, such as cancer and arthritis, are associated with too much acid in the system.

The cholesterol issue

What about cholesterol? The cholesterol issue must also be understood in context of other lifestyle choices. For example, eggs contain enough lecithin to balance the digestion of their own cholesterol content. Unfortunately, in our world today where chickens are raised in chicken houses and are not free range, the lecithin count is lower. I recommend you buy eggs from free-range chickens that are available in many places now. If that is not possible, I recommend proper supplementation with lecithin, pantethine and inositol hexaniacinate, which will help your body to digest these cholesterol molecules. I believe that if eggs were bad for you, it would mean that God is a bad chemist. And the same goes for meats. God did not forbid the eating of meat, so meats are not bad for you. (See Genesis 9:3; 1 Timothy 4:3–4.)

While it is sadly true that meats today are full of chemicals, it is also true that our vegetables are contaminated with chemical poisons, pesticides and other pollutants. Even if you get organically grown vegetables, you cannot control acid rains, polluted air, bacteria, molds and other contaminants. We can't hide from the condition of our world. So it makes much more sense to me to:

- Eat whole foods in a balanced diet

- Supplement with extra vitamins, minerals, enzymes and essential fatty acids

- Exercise regularly

- Drink plenty of water

- Choose to live your life according to basic Bible principles

The body was designed to function in health based on these recommendations. Following this simple protocol will dramatically improve the health of any person. Of course, there are people who have degenerative processes or handicaps, which would limit some of their activities. They would need to have their physician's recommendations and management. There are others who have neglected some of these recommendations more than others. They will need to overachieve in these neglected areas (such as exercise) to get back into balance.

> **A DISEASE CAN ONLY OCCUR WHEN THE RATE OF DAMAGE EXCEEDS THE RATE OF REPAIR.**

Whatever the case, the problem can only be solved by lifestyle choices that activate the processes built into the natural and inherent design and by maintaining that practice for a significant period of time. Consuming the proper balance of protein—meat, eggs and cheese—on a consistent basis is part of that design. This gives the body plenty of essential building blocks (amino acids) to repair, rebuild and replicate the damaged cells that lead to the disease process. A disease can only occur when the rate of damage exceeds the rate of repair. By consuming a proper diet and incorporating the right balance of proteins, you can reverse that process and allow the body's rate of cellular repair to exceed the rate of damage back on the road to recovery.

Understanding Carbohydrates

In the human body, essentially all carbohydrates are converted into glucose by the digestive tract and liver before they reach the cell. Glucose is further metabolized and combined with oxygen to produce ATP (energy). That energy is then made available to be used for the body's many functions. However, while carbohydrates are burned by the body for fuel, they yield less energy to the body than fats do per molecule, as I have mentioned.

Overconsumption of carbohydrates can cause problems for people, especially if they are sensitive to them. Their reactions are not allergic, but metabolic. Individuals with carbohydrate sensitivities dump excessive amounts of insulin into their systems in response to consuming carbohydrates. This extra insulin can trigger a host of unpleasant symptoms (such as fatigue, elevated cholesterol, elevated triglycerides, abnormal craving, cyst formations and yeast overgrowth). The main problem with overconsumption of carbohydrates is that it causes the body to store fat and burn sugar instead, as we discussed in chapter three, "A Society of Carboholics." This condition is caused primarily by poor eating habits.

Proper sources of carbohydrates

Plants manufacture and store carbohydrates as their chief source of energy. Carbon dioxide from the air and water from the soil are joined together in green leaves, where chlorophyll acts as a catalyst, as they incorporate the energy of sunlight to form glucose, a basic carbohydrate. Oxygen is then released from the plant into the air as a by-product. These carbohydrates then form more complex ones, as well as other organic compounds. Humans and animals eat these plants to maintain the compounds necessary for life. God wonderfully designed us to need and enjoy the food from these plants. In the Book of Genesis we read:

> And God said, Behold, I have given you every herb bearing seed, which is upon the face of all the earth, and every tree, in the which is the fruit of a tree yielding seed; to you it shall be for meat.
>
> —GENESIS 1:29

When humans consume plants, the body utilizes the premixed compounds through proper digestion and combines them with oxygen to produce ATP energy. Carbohydrate metabolism is very complex and quite extensive in the explanation of its physiology. This chapter is designed simply to give you a brief overview to help you understand how carbohydrates work in your body.

Basically, when a carbohydrate is digested, it is broken down into sugar molecules. It is then mixed with oxygen and is converted to energy. In order for the glucose molecules to be used, they must be converted into *glycogen*. Once the body begins the breakdown of sugar, the pancreas releases insulin, which enables the glycogen to enter the muscles to be used for fuel. This process is continually occurring throughout the day and is part of the normal human physiology.

Certain B vitamins, amino acids, enzymes, coenzymes and trace minerals such as vanadium and chromium also play an important role in this process. Once again, the problems experienced from consumption of carbohydrates begin once an imbalance occurs. That imbalance can be caused by:

- Eating too many carbohydrates

- Eating the wrong kind of carbohydrates

- By vitamin, mineral and nutrient deficiencies

If you are addicted to carbohydrates (as most Americans are), the first step toward improved health is to break the addiction. Most chronic diet abusers and carboholics have multiple nutritional deficiencies, and implementing strategic supplementation can be just as important as changing the diet. I have listed strategic recommendations in my Protocol D-7 (page 176). If you choose to follow this protocol for eight to ten weeks, you can usually break the addiction.

After the addiction has been broken, it's time to resume a normal healthy diet. I recommend that you follow my Stay Healthy Diet on page 179, which basically instructs you to eat whole foods in their relative proportions. That means simply eating one-hand portions of each of the three categories listed in the protocol at each meal. If after completing a meal you still feel hungry, do not create an imbalance by indulging in a partial portion of a protein or a carbohydrate food. Instead, continue to balance your diet by taking a small portion of each one of the food groups listed until you are satisfied. Remember, you should stop eating when you are still slightly hungry; this will prevent overeating.

Today's diets are full of refined carbohydrates, which not only are void of vital nutrients, but they actually help drive the body toward becoming more deficient. Refined carbohydrates are converted directly to sugar, causing rapid absorption that creates so many unbalanced reactions in the body. The problem with the current diet structure (such as fast foods, processed foods and refined sugars) is that the foods consumed are high in processed sugars that rapidly absorb in the digestive tract, causing the body to release excessive amounts of insulin. It also alters other metabolic hormones (such as glucagon, epinephrine and glucocorticoids) in response to the insulin release. The sudden sugar spikes that are created, followed by a rapid decline in blood glucose, can have detrimental effects on the body over a period of time.

The most common condition I see as a result of high-carbohydrate diets in my own clinic is hypoglycemia (low blood sugar). Individuals suffering from this condition may experience sudden onsets of fatigue, headaches, fainting spells, generalized weakness, low ambition and chronic pain syndromes, especially a couple of hours following their meals. Those who work in a stressful environment are at even greater risk for developing this condition.

Hypoglycemia is caused simply from consuming too many carbohydrates (especially refined ones) and not having enough protein to bring a balance. If these blood sugar levels continue to spike and drop rapidly over a period of time, they usually lead to diabetes. I commonly refer to people who have become diabetics from following this chronic destructive eating pattern as "end-stage carboholics." It is possible to break your carboholic addiction and improve your health by making right lifestyle choices.

Understanding Fats

Essentially all of the cells of your body are lined with *fat*. This is by design. Fat makes the cells permeable for nutrients to pass across the membrane. Substances such as hormones, micronutrients and other vital nutrients must be able to pass through the membrane to enable the cell to survive. The fat serves as a protective barrier, keeping the *outside out* and the *inside in,* while at the same time allowing it to absorb the appropriate substances into the cell. Fat is also used to make prostaglandins, which maintain control of inflammatory processes in the body (swelling and inflammation).

This fat membrane located in every cell is called the phospholipid bilayer. The fats you consume every day turn into cell membranes. Approximately every three months, the total fat you have consumed will have exchanged places with the current phospholipid bilayers. This is a continual cycle. The fluidity and permeability (the ability of membranes to absorb) of the cells is largely determined by the degree of "unsaturation" of the fats in the cell membrane. So the kinds of fats you consume will determine how healthy your cell walls will be. Healthy, unsaturated fats that the body needs are found, for example, in olive oil and safflower oil, as well as other seed oils. In our culture, people are consuming diets high in saturated fats, which means fats that cannot absorb. These fats are found in all processed foods, fast foods, chips, crackers and candies. Just as a sponge that is full of water can no longer absorb liquid, saturated fats that line cell walls can no longer absorb nutrients. This lack of absorption leads to cell deficiency, which results in disease and even death.

When people line their cells with fats converted from saturated fats, instead of the cell walls being pliable and absorbable, they become rigid and unable to absorb. Partially hydrogenated fats produce the same effect on the cell wall as the saturated fats. Partially hydrogenated fats are found in almost all processed foods, chips, crackers and candies. Because these fats are not properly broken down for use by the cell, they often accumulate in the veins and arteries, leading to cardiovascular disease. For this reason I recommend that you avoid saturated and partially hydrogenated oils. Avoid fatty meats, lard, animal fat and any package or box that lists partially hydrogenated oils in its content.

As we learned in our biochemistry lesson, fats break down into essential fatty acids. These fatty acids are then further metabolized to be used for energy, to help mediate inflammatory reactions in the body or to be stored for future use. The majority of these fatty acids are grouped into the omega-6 family and the omega-3 family. Omega-6 oils are found primarily in vegetable oils and grains. Omega-3 oils are found primarily in cold-water fish and flaxseed.

Maintaining appropriate levels of these oils in the body is extremely important, but establishing the balance between the two is the most crucial issue. If the omega-6 to omega-3 ratio becomes too high, it creates an imbalance in the body with some very unpleasant side effects. An imbalance in these vital oils results in a condition that is highly pro-inflammatory and can cause widespread destructive inflammatory reactions throughout the body. Dr. Brad Rachman from Great Smokies Diagnostic Laboratory shared some interesting statistics during a lecture concerning the essential fatty acid ratios and how their delicate balance is currently being upset by our American diet. He noted that in the early 1900s, the average American's diet consisted of a 4:1 ratio of omega-6 to omega-3 fatty acids. Currently, the ratio of omega-6 to omega-3 fatty acids is 45:1.

Can you understand why there are so many degenerative diseases in our culture? Inflammatory bowel disease, autoimmune disease, cardiovascular disease, arthritis, psoriasis, eczema, joint pain and a host of other degenerative processes can all be produced from these imbalances. Almost everything we eat these days contains some form of vegetable oil, which is high in omega-6 content and increases the unbalanced ratio.

We need to find ways to balance the omega-6 oils we are consuming with the omega-3 oils we need. I highly recommend 1 tablespoon (or its equivalent in gel capsules) of flax oil per day. Consuming this amount of omega-3 oils will help to offset the chronic imbalance caused by our current diet structure. Fish oils will also balance the levels of omega-3 in our bodies. It has been my experience that fish oils seem to produce better therapeutic effects for skin conditions and severe arthritic problems than flax does. However, they have also been shown to produce notable increases in blood sugar and sharp declines in insulin secretion in diabetic patients of both type 1 and type 2 diabetes. Therefore, diabetics should be monitored by their physicians while taking fish oil supplements.[2]

Fish oils also become rancid very quickly, so make sure the supplement you choose contains vitamin E, which helps prevent rancidity. Another caution when taking fish oil supplements is that they may reduce clotting abilities. Although this is a rare occurrence, individuals on blood thinners or with a tendency to bleed or hemorrhage should only use fish oil supplements under supervision of their doctor.

Again, as with proteins, it is the imbalance of fats that cause problems for the body. After years of abuse through diet, it may take several months to reap benefits from making healthy choices to use proper fats and avoid the wrong kinds. However, by making the changes that work with the natural healing processes in the body, you are not just masking the symptoms but correcting the cause. This is a more foundational approach to your health care.

Simply avoid saturated and partially hydrogenated oils. Supplement with omega-3 oils, and don't overdo it with grains and the products that contain vegetable oils. This allows the body to take the bad fats in your cell wall layers and convert them back to healthy absorbable ones. Each day you adhere to these recommendations, the natural recuperative mechanisms for healing will be reestablishing in your system, exchanging rigid cell walls for permeable ones.

Adding Vital Enzymes

What are enzymes, and what do they do in the body? Dr. Edward Howell, one of the leading researchers in enzyme therapy, states, "Enzymes are substances which make life possible. They are needed for every chemical reaction that occurs in the body. Without enzymes, no activity at all would take place. Neither vitamins, minerals nor hormones can do any work without enzymes."[3] Think of it this way: Enzymes are the labor force that builds your body, just as construction workers are the labor force that builds your house. You may have all the necessary building materials and lumber, but to build a house you need workers. Workers represent this vital life element, enzymes. In a similar way, you may have all the nutrients—proteins, carbohydrates, fats, vitamins, minerals and so forth—for your body, but you still need enzymes to keep the body "alive and well."

Enzymes also have the ability to cleanse and purify the blood. Consider that parasites, fungi, bacteria and the shells that protect a virus are all made up of protein. The enzyme *protease* breaks down proteins. Since these invaders in our blood system are proteins, it makes sense that ingesting this enzyme would not only break down the good proteins we ingest, but it will also break down the protein invaders. Fat can be broken down by the enzyme *lipase*. It is a proven fact that lipase helps digest fat. If taken orally, it can take stress off the gallbladder, liver and pancreas, which all play a vital role in the breakdown of fats.

Unfortunately, we don't get enough enzymes from the food we eat. One of the main reasons is that enzymes are destroyed at temperatures of 118 degrees Fahrenheit. This means that cooked and processed foods contain few, if any, enzymes. Also, because of packaging and preparation, more enzymes are destroyed. It seems obvious that to be healthy, you must supplement your diet with enzymes. Fortunately, we can purchase these supplements that will assist the body in its vital functions.

Your Cells and Water

Water is by far the most abundant substance that diffuses through the cell membrane. Physiology textbooks teach that the amount of water that ordinarily diffuses per second in each direction through the red cell membrane is equal to about one hundred times the volume of the cell itself. However, during this process, the total volume of water maintained in the cell stays the same. Water makes up approximately 60 percent of the body's total composition. Considering this fact, it shouldn't take much convincing to realize the importance of drinking plenty of pure water.

If adequate water intake is not achieved, the body becomes dehydrated. Considering all of the functions of the body that require water (such as cleansing, energy production and nutrient transport), dehydration of the body can bring with it great consequences. One of the first signs of dehydration is fatigue. I can't tell you how many people I have examined who complained of fatigue; after I instructed them to rehydrate their system, their energy levels were immediately restored. They have exclaimed to me, "Dr. Hannen, I can't believe I have felt run-down for so long and all I needed was some pure water added back into my diet. That seems so simple."

I was doing a health seminar one weekend during which I took blood samples from the conferees. After viewing 128 blood slides under the microscope, I found that 115 of them showed a significant degree of dehydration. After completing the rehydration protocol, most of them returned and reported a dramatic improvement in how they felt. The amazing thing was that almost all of them told me they didn't think they could be dehydrated because they had been drinking plenty of beverages that day. Some were even brave enough to tell me that they thought I was crazy or that something was wrong with my microscope. They didn't think they were dehydrated because they didn't feel bad or tired.

WATER MAKES UP APPROXIMATELY 60 PERCENT OF THE BODY'S TOTAL COMPOSITION.

However, after they rehydrated, they realized how good they were supposed to feel, and they returned to apologize. You may be wondering how someone that has been drinking beverages can get dehydrated. The answer is simple. Most of the beverages that people drink contain dehydrating agents like acids, caffeine or alcohol. This is true of tea, coffee, sodas, beer and wine, for example. They cannot count as water intake. Actually, in most cases, they cause depletion instead of repletion.

The typical gold standard for water intake is a minimum of six 8-ounce glasses of pure water daily. If you are curious and wondering if you might be dehydrated to some degree that may be preventing you from functioning at your best, try these recommendations. First, begin to use the following rehydration protocol:

- Drink 4 ounces of water every hour on the hour while you are awake.
- Do this for three days.
- Drink no other beverages of any type. You must avoid caffeine, sweets, any diet products or diet supplements.
- After the third day, your body should be adequately rehydrated.

After rehydrating your body, you should maintain proper fluids by drinking six 8-ounce glasses of water per day. If you have not been drinking adequate water, you might notice an increased amount of urination. This is normal, even if you find yourself urinating many times throughout the day and into the night. Eventually, your body will restore its proper balance and the excess urination will subside. However, keep in mind, "more water, more urine."

During this three-day rehydration protocol, the body is able to cleanse many of the unwanted toxins out of the body as well as freely transport vital nutrients to many of the deficient cells. Give it a try and see how you do. Keep this in mind. By the time most people are thirsty, they are already partially dehydrated, so don't necessarily wait until you are thirsty to start.

I am often asked what type of water to drink. The most crucial answer is to avoid drinking tap water. Tap water is high in sediment, bacteria and chlorine content. Chlorine is designed to kill bacteria and other harmful microbes. The problem is that it kills both good and bad bacteria. When we ingest chlorinated water, the good bacteria in our digestive systems are destroyed. These bacteria are our first line of defense against foreign invaders. They also assist us by helping us digest our foods for proper assimilation. Because the chlorinated water and antibiotics in our foods kill the good bacteria, they are continually being destroyed. Losing these good bacteria lowers our immunity and our resistance.

One important way to prevent yourself from falling into the disease trap is to avoid chlorinated water. Another is to repopulate good bacteria through supplements. The colon cleansing product I formulated, for example, contains the good bacteria and should be taken on a daily basis to appropriately repopulate the digestive tract.

I highly recommend a reverse-osmosis filter for your home. If you are buying water from the store, make sure it has been through a reverse-osmosis filter (RO) and has been UV light treated. Try to avoid distilled water unless you are in a cleansing process. Distilled water is called "empty water." It has been stripped of all of its nutrient content. Though it can be effective for certain cleansing protocols, because it tends to leach particles with which it comes in contact, distilled water should never be consumed for any prolonged periods of time. If you do, I recommend you add minerals back into your system by taking supplements.

In Conclusion

What we have discussed simply offers as a solution for most ills a very pleasurable prescription: Eat! You may complain that this prescription does not come from a scientific diagnosis. It is too hard to believe that you can give the body the nutrition it needs and all its symptoms will go away. If my answer sounds foolish to you, let me refer to the Bible for my reply. The apostle Paul declared, "God hath chosen the foolish things of the world to confound the wise; God hath chosen the weak things of this world to confound the things which are mighty" (1 Cor. 1:27).

I am "foolish" enough to believe that the body is designed to heal itself. I have built my clinical practice on this and other biblical principles that seem foolish to many who have chosen to embrace the conventional medical philosophy that treats symptoms without getting to the cause of the problem. Yet, it is a simple fact that the body is designed to maintain health and heal itself when it is given the proper nutrients it needs to build health.

Though bacteria, viruses, yeast and a host of other malignant invaders may attempt to interfere with this innate healing process, human cells continue to dominate, and mankind continues to replenish the earth, one cell at a time. The cell, as we have discussed, is the basic unit of life. Cells form tissues, which in turn

> **WHEN TREATING THE BODY, THE FIRST QUESTION SHOULD ALWAYS BE: IS THIS TREATMENT ASSISTING OR INTERFERING WITH THE ORIGINAL DESIGN?**

form organs and bone structure. These ultimately form a meticulous display of complex biochemical and biomechanical systems perfectly organized and synchronized to function in a capacity that far exceeds human comprehension. One of those functions is its innate ability to heal itself.

If you cut the body, it will heal whether or not you exercise faith for healing. Even surgery would not be possible except for the fact the incision made by the surgeon will heal, allowing the skin to close over the wound and protect organs and bone. Healing is built into the original design. The exception to that reality would be if something interferes with the body's natural healing processes.

That is why, when treating the body, the first question should always be: Is this treatment assisting or interfering with the original design? Many treatments and health practices today compromise the health processes of the original design, yet millions of people accept those treatments as "normal" healthcare. Normal healthcare would be to choose the lifestyle God intended us to live, maintaining health simply by feeding our bodies—our cells—the nutrients they need for health.

CHAPTER 6

Cleanse and
Protect the Cell

Environmental pollution is becoming one of the leading topics
of the day. Our current society shows very little concern for the
detrimental effects of this worldwide problem. *USA Today* published an article in May 2000 that stated that more than 132 million
Americans could be at risk for health problems because the com-
munities where they live have dangerously high smog levels. The
article also referenced a 1998 EPA report that said 10 percent of
America's lakes, rivers and bays contain toxic sediment that poses
health risks to aquatic life and humans.[1]

It is not hard to conclude that the body needs immediate assis-
tance against these harmful invaders. These toxic pollutants (xeno-
biotics) have been directly linked to cancer as well as a host of other
diseases and disorders. Although we can't always change the
harmful things around us, by taking proper measures we can
change the way those things *affect* us. Certain antioxidant vitamins
and phytochemicals, which occur naturally in herbs, protect the
body against many of the harmful effects produced by these substances. Taking antioxidant vitamins and certain herbs is a good
preventative step toward protecting your future, as we will discuss.

How Do We Cleanse?

We mentioned earlier the filters your body uses to cleanse itself. Many people are not aware that the body has filters. So they have no idea that we must be responsible to help the body cleanse the filters. For the sake of discussion, let me list your body's five main filtration systems again for you:

1. Your liver is your chemical filter.

2. Your kidneys are your fluid filters.

3. Your lungs and airways are your air filters.

4. Your spleen is your blood cell filter.

5. Your lymphatic system is your intercellular filter.

These five filtration systems dump many of their toxins into the colon. That is why cleansing these filters as well as the colon is vital for our health.

When food is digested, as we have explained, and the body breaks it down into tiny elements to be used by the body for energy, repair and other processes, there are elements of debris collected as well. All of these unwanted leftovers (cellular debris, antigens and other circulating waste) are recycled through the liver, kidneys, spleen and lymphatic system, where they can be properly discarded from the body, usually through the bowel and urinary tract.

If one of these filtering organs or systems is not functioning properly, the entire body may begin to suffer an accumulation of toxins. This can lead to extensive cell damage, symptoms, sickness and disease. It can also prevent the body from absorbing nutrients, thus depriving the cells of proper nutrition. This nutrient deprivation can also lead to deficiencies that produce cell damage, symptoms, sickness and disease. When you understand these fundamental workings of the body, you can see how providing adequate nutrients (such as vitamins, minerals, essential fatty acids and enzymes) and maintaining proper filtration would lead to optimal health, thus greatly diminishing sickness and disease. That is what I call *primary healthcare*.

When we detect a problem with one of our body's filtering systems, we need to find a way to cleanse it. We understand this principle when we think of oil and air filters in our cars, swimming pools and air conditioners. We replace filters or flush them in order to keep the accumulation of waste from choking the life out of these mechanical motors.

While we do not want to think of replacing any of the filters in our body, we can find ways to flush them, removing the overload of toxins that is creating the problem. Just like flushing filters in our mechanical "toys," we need to flush the filters in our body to avoid becoming sick and unhealthy. We want to avoid having waste products like toxins, chemicals, cellular debris, metals, bacteria, yeast and viruses accumulate in these filtering systems.

We have read from Genesis 1:29 that God created herbs to be used by humans to sustain them. In the broad sense, herbs include all growing foods. For centuries, people have known that many herbs have a cleansing effect on the body as well. A good example is prune juice and oatmeal. If a human ingests these herbs, the effect will be a cleansing of the bowels. They are naturally designed to perform that function.

There are specific herbs that cleanse every filtering organ of the body safely and effectively. *Detoxification* is the term used for cleansing toxins out of the system. Herbs have been used safely for thousands of years to detoxify the body. Besides cleansing the body, herbs also offer wonderful healing and repairing potential. For example, a quick application of gel from an aloe plant will bring immediate relief to a burn and often prevent it from blistering.

Some herbs have a healing effect on our filtering organs (liver, kidneys, lungs, spleen and lymphatic system) similar to the way aloe heals our skin. Other herbs also have a protective effect as well. One study showed that rats would die when given a particular poisonous mushroom, but when given an herbal preparation, the rats were no longer affected by the poison.[2] In this particular case the herbal preparation protected the liver, thus preventing death. Herbal preparations can assist the body in three main ways: cleansing, repairing and protecting.

Protecting the Cell

Oxidation is a degenerative process that damages cells in the body. If you have ever seen a shiny piece of steel left out in the weather, which caused it to rust, you have witnessed the result of oxidation. Or perhaps an apple is lying on the counter with a bite taken out of it. In a few minutes, it turns brown. That is also the result of oxidation. Oxidation on a cellular level occurs on a daily basis and is constantly threatening to tear down the cells. Antioxidants ("against oxidation") protect the cells from this destructive process, thus preserving the life of the cells. Spraying zinc spray on a piece of steel will keep it from rusting; sprinkling ascorbic acid (vitamin C) on a fruit salad will keep it from turning brown. Both zinc and ascorbic acid are antioxidants.

THE CELL IS THE MOST BASIC LIVING UNIT OF THE BODY.

Cellular immunity 101

We are constantly bombarded with media reports about a new "scare" that threatens our health or our lives. Recently we have been hearing reports of the possibility of some type of biochemical or biological warfare like anthrax, Ebola or smallpox against which we need to defend ourselves. These reports have caused fear to fill many hearts.

If people simply understood how the immune system works, their fears could be relieved. They would understand how a healthy body fights against these "germs" when it comes into contact with them. I think we should be knowledgeable in case we are somewhat exposed to these biological agents. CNN did a report about an outbreak of anthrax in Russia. The Russians were developing their "germ warfare," and somehow spores of anthrax leaked out, spreading to several towns. Thousands of people were exposed to those "deadly" spores, but only sixty people died as a result of that exposure.[3]

Of course, that is a tragedy. But I am trying to explain that though thousands of people were exposed to anthrax spores, only a few were affected physically. The overriding issue is not exposure to anthrax or any other biological germ; it is the strength of your immune system. The younger, stronger, healthier bodies were able to resist the anthrax spores, and by the time some of them could be examined, the body had already expectorated the spores, putting them into remission. They were completely symptom free.

If I swabbed your throat and took that swab to a microbiology lab to grow those cultures for three or four days, I would discover that you had almost every virus and bacteria known to man residing in your throat. So why aren't you sick? Because there is another phenomenon regarding your body's defense system—the immune system—that doesn't allow those bacteria, viruses and other free radicals to affect your body. What is that phenomenon? Healthy cells.

We understand that the cell is the most basic living unit of the body. Each organ is an aggregate of many different cells held together by intracellular supporting structures. There are from seventy-five to one hundred trillion cells in the entire body, and they are constantly reproducing. If healthy cells are forming healthy organs and healthy organs are forming a healthy body, then you have an individual who is healthy—in a state of wellness. If sick cells are forming sick organs and sick organs are forming a sick body, then you have an unhealthy individual—a diseased individual.

Did you know that most diseases are simply named for the location where damage is occurring in the body? For example, damaged cells in the heart signal heart disease; damaged liver cells signal liver disease, and a damaged gallbladder is gallbladder disease. That means that disease or disorders are based on *the condition of your cells.* That being true, I believe it makes sense to consider how we can protect our cells.

Because our cells are continually reproducing themselves, the body is continually rebuilding itself, either for health or for disease. For example, within three months all of our red blood cells will have been replaced with new ones. If you are producing healthy cells through proper nutrition, your body will replace your current cells with new healthy ones. If you have sick, diseased or injured cells, they are vulnerable cells that will continually reproduce more sick and vulnerable cells.

If this cycle continues, you will always be prone to disease, attacks, viruses, bacteria, infections or whatever condition the "diseased cells" create. Proper nutrition and water help to make our cells resistant to these pollutants entering the body and causing a phenomenon called *free-radical damage*. Free radicals are misformed molecules that cause harmful chemical reactions, which can damage body tissues. That means that through the process of oxidation, the pollutant simply destroys the membranes of your cells, making them vulnerable to disease.

Scientists refer to viruses or bacteria as "opportunists," because if they have an opportunity, they will get you. However, if you keep your cells nourished, cleansed and protected, they stay healthy and do not give opportunity for infections or disease to attack. This simple concept can help you understand the responsibility you have to provide your body what it needs to be healthy. The obvious question we need to answer is this: How do we succeed in producing healthy cells? Or perhaps, How do we protect the healthy cells we have? I am glad you asked.

Scientists often say, for example, that the cause of cancer is unknown. However, I can find posted on various government websites a very long list of chemicals with warnings like: "Chemicals known to cause cancer." You have probably seen the radiation badges worn by workers around radiation areas. At my clinic, we have to wear these badges because if we are overly exposed to x-ray radiation sources, we could get cancer. Electricians who work on high power lines have to wear those badges as well because they are continually exposed to radiation. Given these facts, we can conclude that cancer can be caused by chemicals and radiation. So why do scientists insist that they don't know what causes cancer?

And consider this irony: The conventional treatment for cancer uses chemicals (chemotherapy) and radiation. Go figure! I am not trying to determine whether this treatment practice is right or wrong. I am just saying that it has never made sense to me because I know what chemicals and radiation do to harm a cell. They tear it down and make it more vulnerable. Even technicians who are giving these treatments have to be shielded from the harmful effects of radiation.

I would prefer a treatment that tried to *remove* harmful chemicals from the body rather than adding more that could potentially harm healthy cells. Why not find nutrients that you can put back into the body to make the cells strong and healthy and help the membranes to become resistant to diseases like cancer? Why not use natural compounds that protect the cell from harmful chemicals and radiation, as well as others that help to remove them safely from the body? Doing so would make it almost impossible for cancer, microorganisms, viruses and bacteria to affect the body. Doesn't that make sense to you?

Understanding Antioxidants

My search for answers to those questions listed above drove me to begin studying the immune system and how to strengthen it against the destructive effects of oxidation and other forces. In my search, I began to study a classification of compounds called antioxidants. Just as the rust was formed on the weather-exposed steel as a result of oxidation, so human cells can be destroyed when they are exposed to the environment with no protection. Antioxidants form a protective layering around the cell so that agents or contaminants cannot harm the cell.

Cooks prove this principle every time they sprinkle ascorbic acid powder (vitamin C powder) on fruits and vegetables to keep them from oxidizing, or turning brown. Zinc is another antioxidant that can be sprayed on a steel pole to keep it from rusting. Zinc creates a protective layer around the pole so that oxidation cannot occur. In the same way, when you put antioxidants inside your body, they insulate the cells and form a protective barrier around them against harmful invaders. If you learn to insulate the basic unit of life—the cell—you can possibly keep it protected from anything that will destroy it or make it vulnerable to disease. As you keep it safe and healthy, you increase resistance to disease for the whole body.

Increasing the resistance of a cell is called giving it "immunity." This means the cell has become immune to its harmful environment. The more you protect the cell, the better your body's immunity becomes. In other words, your body will have the ability to resist harmful organisms, viruses and bacteria. And the good news is that these natural antioxidant compounds that give your cells immunity don't cause harmful side effects.

When you are not producing healthy cells, you are prematurely aging. Aging sooner than you should is caused simply by a literal breakdown of cellular health. Your cells are dying, and you are aging. The faster your cells break down, the faster you age.

Antioxidants slow down or reverse the aging process to some degree. They can insulate the cells and keep them healthier, which gives them a higher resistance and a greater immunity. Dr. Ali is one of the foremost experts in the field of alternative and integrated medicine. He was also a twenty-year pathologist in a hospital in Miami and is a very highly respected author. While I was attending postgraduate studies at Capital University of Integrated Medicine, during a lecture he stated boldly that he believes virtually all disease stems from "free-radical damage."[4] The more I study the body, nutrition and nutrition's effect on the body, the more I am convinced that he may be right! Disease is a result of the cell breaking down and becoming vulnerable in any area of the body or any organ where it is formed. If cells are dying in any area, that cell or system or part of the body becomes diseased.

Understanding that our cells are vulnerable to breakdown or death, and knowing that there are natural compounds we can put into our bodies to protect our cells, let's look at a few of them and evaluate the benefits they offer. I encourage you to study more in-depth the entire gamut of antioxidants that can build your immune system and improve your health so dramatically.

Beta carotene

Vitamin A (beta carotene) stimulates and enhances numerous immune processes, including the induction of cell-mediated immunity against tumors. Wouldn't you like to build your cells' resistance to tumors? Beta carotene increases natural killer cell activity. Natural killer cells in the body are like an internal army. They are the soldiers that your body deploys when it's time to fight off an organism that is trying to attack your body. Vitamin A increases that natural killer cell activity and antibody response. It also demonstrates potent antiviral activity, which means it resists viruses. Studies have demonstrated an inverse relationship between the intake of beta carotene and cancer incidents. The higher the intake of beta carotene, the lower the incidents of cancer.[4]

Studies have also shown that beta carotene can increase the frequency of T-helper cells by approximately 30 percent after seven days and all of the T-cells after fourteen days. T-cells play a critical role in establishing the immune status of the cell. The more the T-cells, the better the immunity is for that cell. Studies also show that oral beta carotene is useful for boosting antitumor immunity in cancer patients. So, even for people who are already sick, beta carotene can boost that antitumor effect in their body to keep the sickness from spreading; beta carotene may even improve their condition.[5]

Vitamin C (ascorbic acid)

Vitamin C not only visually affects fruits and vegetables, as we have mentioned, but it also reduces cancer rates, boosts immunity, protects cells against pollution and cigarette smoke, enhances wound repair and even increases life expectancy. It plays a vital role in many immune mechanisms. White blood cells, especially the lymphocytes, have high concentrations of vitamin C. During an infection, white blood cells are fighting to resist it, using up vitamin C. So a vitamin C deficiency may ensue if it is not replenished.

Vitamin C is a proven antiviral and antibacterial. It protects every cell it occupies. You can research the Internet or read materials by Linus Pauling, who has done extensive research on vitamin C. He describes miraculous cases of diseases and degenerative processes that he has turned around by simply prescribing one antioxidant, vitamin C. Vitamin C has stood the test of time.

All antioxidants do the same task; they protect the cell from oxidation. However, some antioxidants perform other wonderful tasks for the body as well. For example, bioflavonoids are often administered with vitamin C because they make it more effective. Not only do they enhance vitamin C, but they are also useful for enhancing the immune system and preventing viral infections. Some also work as an anti-inflammatory, an antiviral, and an anti-allergic agent. They even demonstrate anticancer activity.

Zinc

Zinc is perhaps the most critical nutrient of the immune system because it is involved in so many immune mechanisms. It works not only on the cellular level but also with the thymus gland function and the thymus hormone response. Children who are prone to upper respiratory infections often have low levels of zinc. Zinc inhibits the growth of several viruses, including herpes simplex. It reduces the average duration of colds by seven days and also inhibits the replication of the cold virus. That means it stops the virus in its tracks without allowing it to progress to a more serious condition. This aspect of zinc's benefit is especially important during cold and flu seasons.

Vitamin E and selenium

Vitamin E and selenium are also extremely important in preventing free-radical damage to the cell membranes. Because your membranes and tissues are your first line of defense, if your membranes are damaged, needing repair, they are vulnerable to attack. If you can overcome the attack at the membrane level, then the invader organisms can't penetrate any deeper into the tissues.

Low levels of either vitamin E or selenium put people at high risk of cancer, cardiovascular disease, inflammatory diseases and other conditions associated with increased free-radical damage, including premature aging. Selenium is an antioxidant that shines as a benefit to the heart and to blood vessels. However, its most impressive results are seen in the body's immune system. For example, in one study, selenium supplementation of 200 micrograms daily to individuals with normal selenium concentrations in their blood resulted in a 118 percent increase in the ability of lymphocytes to kill tumor cells and over an 82 percent increase in the important activity of the natural killer cells.[6]

Alpha-lipoic acid and leutine

A compound called alpha-lipoic acid, which is used orally as an antioxidant for diabetes, AIDS, cancer and liver conditions, has also been shown to reduce complications of macular degeneration, or sudden blindness. Medical science says that macular degeneration can't be reversed, so it is important to shield your body with these compounds to make sure that you don't ever get it. One compound that may help to stop the macular degeneration process is leutine. Cataracts and neuropathies are common in both type 1 and type 2 diabetes patients. When neuropathies form, the leg and lower extremities begin to die. Alpha-lipoic acid, leutine and other antioxidants are natural compounds that can help shield the cells and actually assist in bringing life back to those tissues.

Green grasses

Another compound that carries various names is made of tender green grasses or algae. It is rich in B vitamins and helps reduce and keep stress from the cell. It has been shown to increase antibody production, reduce hyperlipidemia, lower liver triglycerides and enhance the protection against the effects of gamma radiation. This compound has also been effective against herpes simplex, cytomegalo virus, mumps, measles, influenza-A and HIV-1. I believe these compounds should be taken into your body every day in adequate doses, not just the token doses that many commercial products supply. Adequate doses are not doses that simply make you feel good; they are clinical doses that you need for protection. Only then will you know that your cells are insulated and protected. When your immunity becomes high, you can have peace that harmful pollutants of the world will not prevail against your body.

Proanthocyanidins (OPCs)

A variety of plant sources yield a family of flavonoids called proanthocyanidins. Often they are chained together (oligomers); hence the name oligomeric proanthocyanidins, or OPCs. Pine bark and grape seeds are typical commercial sources. They have been shown to have cardioprotective effects due to their ability to remove free radicals from the heart muscle.[7]

Ginkgo biloba

Ginkgo biloba increases the flow of oxygen to hypoxic tissues (or tissues that have been choked off by stroke, poor memory, ringing of ears or vertigo) and it is useful for patients with problems of getting oxygen into the proper parts of the brain. Ginkgo compounds help bring that oxygen back to the upper extremity and into the brain. Elderly patients who suffer from senile dementia can benefit greatly by taking ginkgo biloba. It is a strong antioxidant that helps protect brain cells.

While profit-oriented pharmaceutical companies are scrambling to develop vaccines that germ warfare engineers could easily render useless, you can be building stronger, more resistant cells by using compounds manufactured by applying God's design. Remember, the stronger your immune system is, the more protected the cells are, and the less chance you have for infection or disease.

When I formulated the product *Incellate*, I put all of the antioxidants listed above in it. I formulated it with all natural compounds that your body can use to protect itself. My family and I, along with all my friends and loved ones, will take Incellate for the rest of our lives. You don't have to live in fear as many of your neighbors and friends do; instead you can equip your body with these immune-building substances and depend on the divine design that's within you to resist any threat of disease.

Feeding, cleansing and protecting the cells of your body are not an impossible task; it is a responsible one that will insure health for many years. It is my conviction that when we choose to take responsibility for the wonderful design of our bodies and learn to nourish and care for it as God ordained, we will enjoy the health He planned for us to enjoy. Having said that, life does bring many challenges to us that sometimes need special consideration in order to maintain or restore our health. In the next section we will discuss briefly some of these special needs.

SECTION III

SPECIAL HEALTH NEEDS

Bless the LORD, O my soul, and forget not all his benefits:
Who forgiveth all thine iniquities; who healeth all thy
diseases; who redeemeth thy life from destruction; who
crowneth thee with lovingkindness and tender mercies;
who satisfieth thy mouth with good things;
so that thy youth is renewed like the eagle's.

—PSALM 103:2–5

CHAPTER 7

Hormone "HELP!"

When the word *hormone* is mentioned, many people immediately think of estrogen or one of the other sex hormones: progesterone or testosterone. Perhaps that is true because of the media attention given to the controversy in the medical science community over how to treat menopausal women. For some people, the words *hormone* and *estrogen* are almost synonymous. It may surprise them to know that there are three different classes of hormones with several hormones that belong to each category. The body cannot function properly without maintaining hormonal health in every case.

Dorland's Illustrated Medical Dictionary defines a hormone as:

> A chemical substance produced in the body by an organ, cells of an organ, or scattered cells having a specific regulatory effect on the activity of an organ or organs.[1]

In simple terms, hormones are chemical messengers that affect the different ways organ systems function. They can both stimulate or suppress functions of many different systems of the body. Arthur C. Guyton and John E. Hall state in the tenth edition of their *Textbook of Medical Physiology:*

> The multiple hormone systems of the body play a key role

in regulating almost all its functions, including metabolism, growth and development, water and electrolyte balance, reproduction, and behavior. Without growth hormone, a person becomes a dwarf. Without (the hormones) thyroxine and triiodothyronine from the thyroid gland, almost all the chemical reactions of the body become sluggish, and a person becomes sluggish as well. Without insulin from the pancreas, the body's cells can use little of the food carbohydrates for energy. And without the sex hormones, the sexual development and sexual functions are absent.[2]

The list of the many hormones in the body is quite extensive; however, they do fall into three main classifications:

1. *Proteins* and *polypeptides,* including hormones secreted by the anterior and posterior pituitary gland, the pancreas (insulin and glucagon), the parathyroid gland (parathyroid hormone) and many others

2. *Steroids* secreted by the adrenal cortex (cortisol and aldosterone), the ovaries (estrogen and progesterone), the testis (testosterone) and the placenta (estrogens and progesterone)

3. Derivatives of the amino acid *tyrosine* secreted by the thyroid, *thyroxin* and *triiodothyronine,* and the adrenal medullae, *epinephrine* and *norepinephrine*[3]

It is extremely important to health to keep all hormones in the body in balance. Hormones are extremely powerful and are capable of causing serious health conditions if they are disrupted from their proper function. Certain foods, chemicals, physical activities, emotional reactions, stresses, temperature changes and a host of other forms of stimuli can cause significant changes in the sensitive and delicate balance of these powerful chemical mediators. Although estrogen and progesterone seem to have received the majority of the notoriety more recently, the other hormones listed are equally important to our health. In this chapter we will discuss natural ways to preserve hormonal balance.

Women's Hormonal Issues

In my clinical practice I have examined many women who have many of the same major complaints. Sometimes so many complaints are alike that it is difficult to name their specific condition. Typical complaints would be a combination of the following:

- Constant fatigue with no stamina: "I have no energy."

- Symptoms of depression, mood swings, anxiety and crying spells for no reason

- Trouble with insomnia or, if sleeping, feeling like the mind is racing so that the person is not rested when she awakes in the morning

- Difficulty getting out of bed in the morning, sometimes feeling better, however, after breakfast and some movement

- An extremely sleepy spell about an hour after lunch, with loss of mental concentration

- General malaise, brain fog, forgetfulness, especially short-term memory; shopping for groceries and returning home to find that most of the items on the grocery list were forgotten; going to a room in the house to look for something and forgetting what it is

- Difficulty dealing with stress

- Suffer from constipation, indigestion, heartburn and acid reflux

- Experience night sweats, hot flashes, irritability, vaginal dryness and lack of sex drive

Even though many of the women's complaints were the same, their medical exams showed different imbalances. For example, some patients had decreased thyroid levels. Others showed lowered estrogen and progesterone levels. Still others had neither of these test results, but showed adrenal hormone insufficiencies. Though I was mystified by these patients who had similar symptoms and yet showed different test results, I had a gut feeling that there was one common denominator underlying the majority of these health complaints.

Many of my patients had previously been to their family physicians who had given them a wide range of prescriptions, including Zantac and Prilosec to assist with the indigestion; Synthroid or Levothroid to assist with underactive thyroids; estrogen supplementation to assist in hormone imbalances; a variety of laxatives to assist with the constipation; and antidepressants such as Zoloft, Paxil and Prozac to help control the symptoms of depression. I realize that on a short-term basis a lot of these women might have needed some of these medications. However, in the bigger picture, each one of the medications named appeared to be only treating symptoms without addressing the cause of the problem.

Those women who suffered fatigue problems for prolonged periods of time would also develop chronically tight and painful muscle pains, especially in the neck, shoulders and mid-back region. When they visited their family doctor, they would receive a diagnosis of chronic fatigue syndrome or fibromyalgia. It amazes me that so many women come into my clinic with a long list of diagnosed health "symptoms" and a different prescription for each one. Some of these symptoms include hypothyroidism, estrogen imbalance, dyspepsia, indigestion, acid reflux, chronic constipation, anxiety, depression, bipolar disorder, housewife syndrome, high blood pressure, chronic fatigue syndrome and, finally, fibromyalgia.

Researching the cause

Because I understood how the body's metabolism works, I knew there must be an underlying *cause* for all of these symptoms. Treating the cause would help the body to heal itself, and prescription drugs would not be needed to mask the symptoms. I spent hundreds of hours researching the problem and consulted with medical mentors, as well as a variety of healthcare practitioners, some of whom have been practicing clinically over fifty years. Slowly I began to piece together the puzzle to find what was the deficiency of the body and what it needed to regain health and eliminate the symptoms that were common to so many women.

I found that not only was there a deficiency, but there was also excess of certain compounds in these women's diets that produced the deficiency. Because of the delicate hormonal balance of the body, these deficiencies and excesses created disruptions to hormonal function, causing other systems to become deficient in their responsibilities and activities. For example, when the thyroid becomes deficient or suppressed, the whole system becomes sluggish. Other hormones have similar negative effects on different systems of the body they are supposed to regulate. That began to explain the multiple symptoms of which these women complained.

In order to balance body chemistry effectively, it would be necessary to address all hormonal systems. For example, adrenal hormones are most affected by stress, thyroid hormones are most affected by poor diet and lack of exercise, and sexual hormone imbalances are usually created from too much estrogen (or the wrong type) or not enough progesterone in the system. Pancreatic hormones, such as insulin, seemed to be upsetting the apple cart because of the constant stimulation from carboholic eating habits.

Sorting all this out in context of the divine design for the body's intricate hormone balance, it was not difficult to understand how so many women became prisoners in their own body, suffering from multiple symptoms and disorders. Poor lifestyle choices and eating habits contributed to their "disease." The answer to their complaints would involve investigating these issues to see what was stimulating their system to create these imbalances. When the women identified particular habits, determined to make behavior modification lifestyle changes and committed to exercise and proper nutrient supplementation, the cause of their distress could be addressed. They could resolve the underlying health problem instead of just chronically treating the symptoms.

10 THINGS WOMEN NEED TO KNOW ABOUT ESTROGEN

1. Many women are estrogen dominant (have too much estrogen), not estrogen deficient.

2. Estrogen dominance is produced in premenopausal women because of ovulation or lack of ovulation, followed by insufficient production of progesterone.

3. Estrogen dominance is produced in perimenopausal women (ages thirty to mid-fifties) due to erratic cycles or lack of ovulation, when estrogen levels fluctuate rapidly from high to low in the absence of adequate progesterone.

4. Estrogen dominance is produced in postmenopausal women from an excess of estrogen to progesterone ratio. In waning reproductive years when ovarian production of estrogen declines by 40 to 60 percent, progesterone levels can drop to nearly zero.

5. Estrogen dominance can lead to lowered thyroid function, causing cold intolerance (hands and feet are always cold, low body temperature), depression, anxiety, decreased libido, hair loss, evening fatigue and acne.

6. Some women have high levels of xenoestrogens (toxic estrogen that is produced from chemicals in our foods, especially meat and dairy, that have biochemical structures that mimic estrogen).

7. Cholesterol is converted into sex hormones (progesterone, estrogen and testosterone).

8. Adrenal hormones (cortisol and DHEA) can affect the balance of estrogen.

9. Unlike progesterone, which is a single hormone, estrogen is actually used as a general name to represent up to twenty different female hormones of like structure and function. Estrone, estriol and estradiol are the most researched and appear to be the most important types.

10. The worst type of estrogen is estradiol (E2), yet most hormone replacement therapies (HRT) consist of high levels of this kind of estrogen, with low levels of the other types that are shown to be beneficial.

Findings From HRT

Let's take a look at what some doctors are realizing from clinical practice concerning synthetic estrogen therapies. Adding hormones to the body can upset the delicate balance of its own hormone system, with devastating results. The following quotations highlight the current information that is available.

Endometriosis

- Majid Ali, M.D. calls endometriosis "a painful, often disabling disorder that can lead to infertility." He blames estrogen's "overdrive" as the cause for "growth outside the uterus of misplaced cells that normally line the uterine cavity."[4]

Immunity

- Dr. Raymond Peat: "The thymus gland is the main regulator of the immune system. Estrogen causes it to shrink, while progesterone protects it."[5]

Hot flashes

- Dr. Leta Lee: "I have never seen a menopausal woman (whether natural or surgical) who did not successfully ameliorate hot flashes with progesterone treatment."[6]

PMS

- Niels H. Lauersen, M.D.: "When natural progesterone drops, the normal conversion by the adrenal glands cannot take place, salt may build up, fluid may be retained, and hypoglycemia may ensue. Synthetic progestins generally make PMS symptoms worse, so if a woman is about to be treated with progesterone, she should be sure that it is natural progesterone."[7]

Premenstrual epilepsy

- Dr. Katharina Dalton: "One of the most satisfying experiences is to diagnose and treat a woman with premenstrual epilepsy. She can be treated with natural progesterone and freed from all anti-convulsion tablets with their many and unpleasant side effects."[8]

Miscarriages

- Dr. Raymond Peat: "My dissertation research, which established that an estrogen excess kills the embryo by suffocation, and that progesterone protects the embryo by promoting the delivery of both oxygen and glucose, did not strike a responsive cord in the journals which are heavily influenced by funds from the drug companies."[9]

Hysterectomy

- With estrogen so commonly prescribed, Dr. Lee confirms that within a year after taking estrogen a Pap smear will often indicate cervical dysplasia, "soon followed by a hysterectomy. I consider this medical malpractice," he says, "but it happens to hundreds of women every day."[10]

In Summary

It is sad that many women have been following a system that actually leads them to the progression of disease to ultimately end in the castration process, or removing the reproduction glands. Why does the conventional medical system continually push synthetic estrogens when the addition of natural progesterone to the system has proved extremely beneficial in most women? Why does the current establishment continue to frighten our women, leading them to believe that using these synthetic hormones can reduce their risk for disease and improve their general health, when scientific research shows quite the contrary?

The answer is not difficult to find. I think the authors of the book *The Estrogen Alternative* said it best: "Unfortunately, natural substances themselves are not able to be patented and, therefore, do not yield the large profit margins of proprietary drugs."[12]

Most women have been taught to believe that when they have hormonal symptoms, the reason is that they are low on estrogen. The truth is that many women are actually estrogen *dominant;* the levels of estrogen, sometimes the wrong kinds, are too high in their systems. These harmful estrogens are *xenoestrogens* (toxic estrogen) or *estradiol.* The hormones prescribed for most women are extremely high in estradiol, which leads to many side effects.

For thousands of years women have survived without synthetic hormones. Synthetic hormones are not in the original design. Nature provides us with both natural phytoestrogens and phytoprogesterones, which can be used effectively instead of synthetic compounds. However, before administering any type of hormone supplementation to the body, I highly recommend that you have your hormone levels tested (both male and female).

If additional hormone therapy is required, I recommend that you use natural substances. For progesterone you can use dioscoria creams or bio-identical progesterone creams (slightly altered in the laboratory for better conversion). For natural estrogens, I recommend black cohosh, dong quai and isoflavones. For herbs that have a balancing effect to the hormones, I recommend chaste berry, false unicorn and pregnenolone. These provide the best results when taken in combination formulas. There are many formulas on the market today that combine all of these into one capsule or tablet.

For specific salivary and urine specimen hormone testing, these labs are recommended:

- ZRT Laboratory
  1815 NW 169th Place, Suite 5050
  Beaverton, OR 97006
  Phone: 503-466-2445
  www.salivatest.com

- Great Smokies Diagnostic Laboratory
  63 Zillicoa St.
  Asheville, NC 28801
  www.gsdl.com

CHAPTER 8

Design for
Beating Stress

The scientific definition of stress is "the result produced when a structure, system or organism is acted upon by forces that disrupt equilibrium or produce strain." In healthcare the term denotes the physical forces (gravity, mechanical force, pathogen, injury) as well as psychological forces (fear, anxiety, crisis, joy) exerted over the lives of individuals. It is generally believed that biological organisms require a certain amount of stress in order to maintain their well-being. However, when stress occurs in quantities that the system cannot handle, it produces pathological changes that can negatively affect a person's health.

This biological concept of stress was developed by the late Hans Selye. He intended originally for the term *stress* to indicate *cause* rather than *effect*. But through a linguistic error, he gave the term *stress* to effect and later had to use the word *stressor* for the cause.[1] If stress is extreme, unusual or long lasting, the stress response can be overwhelming and quite harmful to a person's system.[2] In each of our daily lives we encounter multiple stresses that affect the body in a variety of ways.

Physical stresses include lifting, exercising, carrying bags and packages and doing other physical labor or activities that require exertion of physical energy. *Environmental* stresses include heat,

107

cold, wind, exposure to chemicals, electromagnetic devices, radio waves, light rays or electrical fields, as well as changes in barometric pressure in our environments. *Emotional* stresses include pressures and anxieties that are work related or relational. *Mental* stresses involve anxiety, confusion, restlessness and other pressures; mental stresses are also related to emotional stresses.

The world around us is constantly providing stimuli that affect the body in ways that cause us stress. The type and amount of stress and our response to it usually determines the outcome that the body will suffer as a result of what it has experienced. When the body reacts a certain way to stressful stimuli, that reaction is referred to as *the stress response.* The stress response is actually part of a larger response known as the *general adaptation syndrome,* a term coined by the pioneering stress researcher Hans Selye.

To understand fully how to combat stress, it is important to understand the general adaptation syndrome. This response to stress involves three phases: *alarm, resistance* and *exhaustion.*[3] You may be aware that when the body responds to stress, it reacts in one of two ways, commonly called the *fight-or-flight response,* which corresponds to the alarm phase. This response is a result of the body activating the sympathetic nervous system.

Typically, the body's autonomic (automatic) nervous system is maintaining an equal balance between sympathetic and parasympathetic tone. The sympathetic system causes a fight-or-flight response when stimulated. The parasympathetic system causes relaxation and tends to promote positive bodily functions such as digestion and other activities that are better performed in a relaxed state. Together these two facets of the nervous system work together to help manage the body, maintaining an even balance as we encounter situations and challenges throughout our day.

Consider the body's attempt to provide this even balance in the following scenario. You are rushing through your busy day, stimulating the sympathetic nervous system to accomplish all your goals. At lunchtime, you rush down to your favorite restaurant to gulp down a sandwich, chips and a soda before running back to the office. Shortly after returning to work, you begin to feel sleepy and sluggish. That is because the body is attempting to stimulate the parasympathetic nervous system, responsible for relaxation, in order to digest properly the food you just gobbled.

This simple explanation of the body's continual working to create balance shows why we need to take time to relax during the day, especially when we are feeding our bodies. Doing this would relieve many digestive problems that are chronic for so many in our society. Problems like acid reflux, dyspepsia, ulcers, irritable bowel syndrome and a host of other digestive disorders are not cured by treating symptoms with over-the-counter medications so highly advertised as the answer. These disorders will be cured by respecting the body's built-in functions designed to maintain health when properly utilized.

Besides failing to honor the body's need for relaxation, another way we violate the body's balance is by burning the proverbial candle at both ends. For example, many corporations are hiring fewer people to carry much heavier workloads, causing increasing stress for employees. The fatigue caused by this over-activity of the body and mind forces the body to react to the stress. The immediate reaction is the fight-or-flight response, which causes the brain and ganglionic systems to excrete hormones and other neuronal chemicals, causing certain changes in the body. The adrenal glands (located on top of the kidneys) are the most commonly affected. When stimulated, they produce adrenaline and other stress-related hormones, causing the body to increase many of its vital functions. The heart tends to race. Sweat production tends to increase, and blood sugar levels rise to prepare the body's muscles for more immediate energy.

This alarm stage of stress response is OK for brief and sporadic episodes because it provides the body with a safeguard so that it can react appropriately to urgent or emergency situations. However, when you continue to burn the candle at both ends, stressing the body for prolonged periods, your body is forced into the second phase of the stress cycle—*resistance,* which is better suited for handling prolonged stress. At this point, more hormones, such as cortisol and other cortical steroids, are released, which help usher the body into the resistance stage. These hormones build larger energy supplies to help the body maintain its functions during a prolonged state of stress. They also make the body retain sodium in an effort to elevate blood pressure. This aspect of stress response is the *major cause for many cases of high blood pressure.* Many people refrain from eating salt in an attempt to lower blood pressure, when, in fact, salt is not the issue. The problem is the release of more hormones to handle new levels of stress.

If the body is continually stimulated to accelerated levels of stress and no lifestyle changes are made to give the body the rest it needs, it will finally shift into the last phase of the stress cycle—the *exhaustion* phase. This response to stress is often referred to as "burnout" or "breakdown." The body has continued to fight to maintain proper balance by producing the hormones responsible for that balance until the adrenal glands and other bodily functions become exhausted.

It is not difficult for me, as a physician, to observe people in a shopping mall who appear to be functioning close to this exhaustion phase. They push themselves all week long, most likely without proper nutrition, while their body fights for survival, keeping the vital functions on an even keel. By the weekend, they are exhausted, but instead of resting, they decide to play the "weekend warrior," further exhausting the body.

And our society's penchant for "fast" food that facilitates our hurried schedules affects not only what people eat, but also how they eat it. They barely chew their food in their hurry, choosing to wash it down with a sugary, caffeinated beverage that further dilutes the digestive juices trying to do their work. Caffeine and sugar replace the energy producers that would build up the body, such as protein and the right kinds of carbohydrates and fats.

Looking for ways to escape the stress of the day, they sit up late at night watching TV or surfing the Internet, losing the hours of rest they need to replenish the body's energies. Even the kind of entertainment many people choose stresses the body. The programming they watch involves violence, terror, murder, bloodshed, loud noises, screams, shrieks, collisions and trauma. People are continually receiving these mental impulses on a regular basis without realizing that the body interprets all of it as stress.

The body was designed to work hard, but it was also designed to rest and to heal. If the body consistently receives the proper amount of rest, it will have adequate time to heal. Then the body is prepared for the work you face the next day. The problem is that in our "microwave society," everything moves at such a fast pace that it appears to be nonstop, and the body never gets a chance for rest or recovery from the continual stimuli that place stress on it.

At my clinic we do a variety of adrenal function tests during which we test individuals' bodies to see how they respond to stress. These tests include a physical examination as well as laboratory tests. I am sorry to say that the majority of my patients, when tested, show some form of adrenal fatigue. The ones who have the most problems seem to have the greatest amounts of stress responses along with chemical imbalances from the hormone reactions that have occurred in their bodies. Their bodies are screaming for rest, simply allowing them to slow down so they can recover and heal.

If we are not willing to address the issue of stress in our lives, and if we insist on overloading our systems with dietary, physical, mental and emotional stressors, without allowing the body time to recuperate, we will soon experience health problems and symptoms of disease. We need to respect our body as the temple of the Holy Spirit and avoid the world system that violates the divine design for our health.

As we discuss the issue of depression, we will learn that sometimes depression is no more than a body that is suppressed from the kinds of stress we have discussed. As you read, I trust you will continue to open your mind and heart to accept the challenge to reevaluate your lifestyle in order to restore health to your body, mind and spirit.

CHAPTER 9

Design for Beating Depression

When I first started working with patients who suffered from depression, I assumed they were victims of an emotional or mental condition. Thousands of men and women (and even children) in America suffer symptoms of depression. I have since concluded that there are three separate conditions that are sometimes diagnosed as "clinical depression." While true clinical depression is a very serious condition that is best addressed by professionally trained psychologists and psychiatrists, especially when a patient is suffering from thoughts of suicide or murder, the other two conditions that mimic depression can be identified and treated by more natural means.

Along with my clinical training, I sought for answers from the Scriptures for my patients with symptoms of depression. I wondered why they were suffering from feelings of sadness, despair and discouragement. Unfortunately, many Christians, sitting in churches with smiles on their faces, exhibit symptoms of depression when they come into my clinic. Many do not realize they are depressed or that they may exhibit symptoms of less severe, though related conditions. Some who do realize their condition fail to address it, perhaps out of fear that they cannot find the help they need.

I want to share with you answers I have found that have worked for my patients. Though medical science has declared depression to be a "disease," I believe the physical condition it creates is only an outward reflection of a deep inner problem. This chapter is devoted to help those who acknowledge they suffer from symptoms of depression, yet do not have an answer to alleviate those symptoms. I want to help you walk away from this misery.

First, let's look at two conditions that mimic depression, causing some of the same symptoms. I will call them, respectively, *suppression* and *oppression*.

Suppression

Suppression can be defined as "prohibiting or stopping activities; to exclude from consciousness; to keep from giving vent to."[1] For example, as relating to the body, when people eat foods that give less energy than the body needs to fulfill all of its functions, the body begins to suppress some normal activities in order to accomplish those that are vital to life. In our discussion of our carboholic society, we learned that burning carbohydrates gives the body two and a quarter times less energy than burning the right kinds of fats. A continual carboholic lifestyle causes the body to suppress activities for which it does not have enough energy.

How do you suppose you would feel if I took away two and a quarter times the amount of energy your body needed? Tired? Fatigued? Depressed? Perhaps. But reality would be that your body is simply suppressed, affecting your brain and even your emotions so that you think negative thoughts and have sad feelings. Remember our definition? Anything that causes the body to suppress or block activities creates a deficiency, which affects the whole body.

Because your diet is your energy source, it will be helpful to understand how certain foods actually contribute to your body's deficiency. Some foods overstimulate the body to expend its energies. These stimulating foods work like a drug. They create the desired immediate result of increased energy, but they do so at a devastating cost to the body. Eating these foods can deplete the body's energy by pressing it into exhaustion. The adrenal glands can become excessively stimulated, pumping adrenaline into the body, especially when it is continually fed starch, sugar, caffeine and other stimulants.

Everyone knows what it feels like to get your adrenaline pumping. When the situation calls for it, that is a good thing. However, excessive stimulation causes these glands to go through a stressful reaction called the *general adaptation syndrome.* As we mentioned in the chapter on stress, this cycle goes through three phases: alarm, adaptation and exhaustion. Eating the wrong food can quickly push the body to the third phase of this cycle: exhaustion. When people reach this stage or get close to it, they experience extremely low energy levels because of the suppression the body is forced to do to maintain its most vital functions.

In the body, energy priorities are very exact. The body knows that first of all, the heart has to beat. Other vital organs, like the liver, have to function; the lungs have to breathe. These vital functions are the body's first priority when it comes to dispersing whatever energy is available. If that energy reserve is used up before other body activities like building the immune system, facilitating mental functions and performing physical activity are accounted for, these deficiencies result in suppression, which causes all kinds of symptoms.

Simple activities like walking up the driveway to get the mail can make you feel winded. You can hear a telephone number and forget it a few seconds later. Perhaps you feel spaced out or experience brain fog. Symptoms such as fatigue, malaise, feeling melancholy, low ambition, lack of motivation, high blood pressure, insomnia and extreme tiredness first thing in the morning or shortly after eating can result from the body's suppression. Acid reflux, constipation, dull headaches (especially at the base of the skull and temples), chronic sinus problems, feeling light headed or faint upon quickly standing up can all be caused from the system being suppressed.

If you think you have been suffering from depression because you have some of these symptoms, I recommend that you give your body a chance to overcome its suppressed state by avoiding the following food stimulants and histamines. You may be surprised at how quickly you respond to a few dietary changes and how much brighter your outlook on life becomes.

AVOID THESE FOODS

Stimulants have the following negative effects on the body:

- They decrease thyroid functions, immunity and energy supply.
- They increase cravings, insulin production and adrenal stress.

Food stimulants that should be avoided include:

- Sugar and sugary foods
- Refined grains (corn starch, corn syrup, white flour, white rice)
- Any form of crackers, chips, white bread
- Chocolate
- Coffee
- Tea
- Fruit juices
- Honey
- Syrups (corn, molasses)
- Preserves and jellies

Excitotoxins are substances that overstimulate nerve cells to the point that they degenerate and even die. Excitotoxins have a profound effect on the brain and nervous system. Some sources for excitotoxins are items containing:

Monosodium glutamate
Hydrolyzed vegetable protein
Hydrolyzed protein
Hydrolyzed plant protein
Plant protein extract
Sodium caseinate
Calcium caseinate

Yeast extract
Textured protein
Autolyzed yeast
Hydrolyzed oat flour
Aspartame, an artificial sweetener (NutraSweet)

L-cysteine (sulfur-containing amino acid; not to be confused with N-acetyl L-cysteine (NAC), which is a powerful antioxidant that helps the body by converting to glutathione)[2]

Histamine foods are foods that produce or contain histamine and produce allergic reactions in some people. Some of the more common histamine foods include:

Sausage	Seafood	Strawberry	Papaya
Sauerkraut	Preserves	Chocolate	Nuts
Tuna	Spinach	Potato	Alcohol
Wine	Tomato	Bananas	Cabbage
Cheese			

Suppression of the body can be easily treated by making a few healthy lifestyle choices. The results will be a marked alleviation of any symptoms of low energy and depression as the body is able to up-regulate and regain the energy it needs from proper nutrition. Along with being free from foods that deplete it through overstimulation, the body will once again prioritize its activities and be able to meet the reasonable demands you place upon it.

Another condition that resembles depression is called oppression. This condition can also be improved with nutritional protocols, but it has some spiritual factors that must be addressed as well. While suppression is based in the body's needs, oppression is based on mental and emotional issues.

Oppression

The definition of *oppress* is "to weigh down with cares or unhappiness."[3] Cares and unhappiness! What are the causes of so much worry today? Why are so many people so unhappy? Do worry and the cares of life cause unhappiness, or does unhappiness contribute to worry? Or both?

When Jesus told His parable of the sower who sowed his seed—the Word of God—into different kinds of soil, one place the seed fell was among thorns. And Jesus said that the thorns were like cares of the world that choked out the seed:

> And the cares of this world, and the deceitfulness of riches, and the lusts of other things entering in, choke the word, and it becometh unfruitful.
>
> —MARK 4:19

When the Word becomes unfruitful in our lives, we cannot receive all the wonderful promises God gives us for abundant life or hope and a future (John 10:10; Jer. 29:11). Instead, our minds become obsessed with the cares of life and the worry that haunts us. We become oppressed in our minds and emotions. The Scriptures teach us how to get rid of these cares: "Casting all your care upon him; for he careth for you" (1 Pet. 5:7). Life will present us with troubles, but instead of allowing them to oppress our minds, we have a remedy that will set us free as we learn how to manage better our mental and emotional states.

Most oppressed individuals that I encounter are quite easy to diagnose. They are full of negative comments, have a pessimistic outlook and radiate their unhappiness by the critical nature they display. Many times I can literally feel this oppressive force from people, almost like a tangible force being transmitted from them. The Bible is clear about the fact that our thoughts and our words are powerful for life or for death:

> Death and life are in the power of the tongue: and they that love it shall eat the fruit thereof.
>
> —PROVERBS 18:21

There is that speaketh like the piercings of a sword: but the tongue of the wise is health.

—PROVERBS 12:18

Over time the strong, oppressive force behind the negative words and thoughts seems to deteriorate the health of these people. It resembles a disease that slowly sucks the life out of their existence. What spawns this type of behavior? What generates the negative thought processes in the minds of these people? What makes them so critical in their evaluation of people and events? Through years of ministry, counseling and treating thousands of patients I have found that there are three major factors that allow oppression to enter your life: *affliction, conflict* and *addiction.*

An individual may have one, two or all three of these factors working in their psyches in combination. However, it has been my experience that many times these factors flow from one to another in sequence. Usually, when a person's body is afflicted or distressed, their mind begins to be conflictive and stressed, which often leads to addiction of some kind in an attempt to find relief. On the other hand, it is possible for mental stress to be the trigger for physical reactions. A closer look at affliction and conflict will help us understand how we arrive at addiction, whether that be to drugs, food, sex, people or any number of other common addictions. Understanding how these three factors are involved in oppression will reveal some of the reasons we feel depressed.

Affliction

The psalmist understood the plight of people in mental torment when he declared:

Again, they are [di]minished and brought low through oppression, affliction, and sorrow.

—PSALM 107:39

Our minds are like highly evolved computers that record, process and retrieve information as it is needed. Every memory that we have experienced or learned helps to form our outlook on life and our expression. Many times in counseling patients, I learn of unresolved issues that cause them guilt, remorse, anger, anxiety and constant inner turmoil. They are haunted by the thoughts and visual images that their minds have recorded. The heart becomes burdened, hardened and callused because of the pain and unresolved anger people carry with them throughout their lifetime. When these people lash out at others, they are really reflecting their own emotional inadequacies.

Many have been victims of abuse in a variety of ways: verbal, sexual, physical, mental, chemical, emotional and even nutritional. All of these factors lead to affliction, simply defined as pain, distress and misery. In turn, affliction causes more pain, distress and misery. In order to achieve healing, the underlying cause of the distress must be determined. These conditions (pain, distress and misery) are simply outward symptoms of internal issues that must be addressed.

Key to release: forgiveness

I personally know of one physician who has been treating cancer patients for over thirty years. One day, in conversation with him, he told me that of all the cases he had treated successfully, each had one or more issues to which they had to apply forgiveness. He went on to say that he had never seen a more destructive force on the human body than the root of bitterness. I have personally witnessed this phenomenon in my own practice, having completed over one hundred thousand patient visits.

Thousands of my patients suffering with different pain syndromes and a variety of diseases seemed to be struggling with deeper issues of mind and heart. I would watch them week after week coming into my clinic wrestling with struggles from the past that wore them down and threatened to cripple their future. I believe that most people suffering from oppression have issues of unforgiveness they need to resolve. If you are suffering from affliction, it is important that you determine the cause of your inner pain and look for those who may need your forgiveness. Forgiving others the things they have done to you will set you free from your inner conflict. It will set you free from your past. Forgiveness will open the door of your heart to the healing power of God who can restore you to peace and health.

Whether you were hurt by a father, mother, sister, brother, aunt, uncle, grandfather, grandmother, cousin, nephew, niece, best friend, stranger, man, woman, girl or boy—forgive them. The pain that has bound you for years can be released in a moment of forgiveness. It is possible that the person you need to forgive the most may be yourself. It does not matter if it was your fault or not. It does not matter the circumstances or who was involved. Let it go. The act of forgiveness is just like deleting a file in your computer. When you choose to do it, the file is gone forever. If you fail to do this, your inner struggles will continue to pop up on the screen of your mind, causing you to make decisions based on wrong information.

For example, if you were involved in an abusive relationship in your past, when Mr. or Miss "Right" comes along, you could find yourself keeping them at arms' length. You can't let them get too close to you because they are saying the same things the abusive person used to say that lured you into their trap. So, as a result, you push them away, even though they have the potential to love you and make your life fruitful. Why? Because you judge them based on a file in your mind that should have been deleted. There are so many good people who are sincere in the things they say and do. Their motives are pure. Yet, when you hold unforgiveness toward a person, it makes you suspect many other people.

Consider the logic in holding people hostage to your unforgiveness. When you cut your finger, it is usually sore for a few days, or if it is a serious cut, a few weeks. But eventually, it heals. You probably would not find yourself continually reliving the circumstances that resulted in your cutting your finger. Years later, would you still be angry for cutting your finger? Of course not; that would be ridiculous. However, many of us refuse to forgive emotional wounds, not allowing them to heal. I know individuals who have harbored anger for thirty to forty years. They embraced a victim mentality that refused to allow a wound to heal and be forgotten. Seeing yourself as a victim puts you on a path of unending pain and misery. Begin to see yourself as a victor, and allow God to bring healing and comfort to your wounds. Jesus declared:

> The Spirit of the Lord is upon me, because he hath anointed me to preach the gospel to the poor; he hath sent me to heal the brokenhearted, to preach deliverance to the captives, and recovering of sight to the blind, to set at liberty them that are bruised.
>
> —LUKE 4:18

Let me mention, as well, that some people who suffer affliction find its source to be a physical stimulus, such as physical pain or irritation. As physicians, we are aware of the effects long-term pain can have on the body. Because of the amount of energy that is expended by the body to deal with inflammatory and spastic reactions, for example, the body is often drained of its energy. This causes suppression of the body, as we have discussed. However, this suppression is caused from a physical affliction. Whatever the form of affliction in your life, it is important to address it and to determine to make the hard choices necessary to eliminate it in order to relieve symptoms of depression.

The second factor in affliction involves mental and emotional conflict, often as a result of stress from our modern-day lives.

Conflict

Conflict is defined as a struggle or battle. A common cause for today's struggles and battles, causing various degrees of unhappiness, is *stress*. Stress can result from anything that causes pressure, tension or strain on the mind and body. When people have exerted all their energies to a task for a length of time, they appear washed out, sometimes with dark circles under their eyes, and even suffer personality changes. They become irritable and short tempered and can be overwhelmed very easily. They worry about everything, especially how they can please the people close to them. Stress makes people become easily distracted from tasks and causes them to have trouble completing them.

Suffering a lack of purpose

We discussed the effects of stress on the mind and body in the previous chapter. I want to share here what I believe is the inner key to much of the stress that people suffer today. It is my conviction that many people are stressed by life events because they lack a sense of purpose for their lives. They search for meaning in endless activities or in overachieving, pursuing possessions, professions or positions. The fact is that everyone needs to have purpose in life to enjoy happiness. God made each of us to fulfill a personal destiny, and, sometimes unconsciously, people are stressed because they are not finding their purpose in life.

One of the first things to consider if you are living in inner conflict is whether you have attempted to discover your purpose for life—your destiny. What did God put you on this earth to do? To find your purpose, you have to begin to acknowledge God in your life. The Bible says that Jesus is the Author and Finisher of your faith (Heb. 12:2). I recommend that you go to your Creator who designed you to be effective in life in a specific way. God did not place you here to be an "oxygen thief"; He has a plan and a specific destiny for your life. You do not have to be talented, gifted or a genius. He just wants you to be available.

I am sure you have observed very successful people who have money, fame, talent and good looks and are intelligent and gifted; yet their lives are in shambles. They appear successful yet live in the epitome of unhappiness. Consider Elvis Presley, for example. What happened to him? How could someone with so much charisma, fame and wealth be so sad, living with addictions to drugs and alcohol? I believe the answer is that people can never be satisfied with things, fame or whatever they seek apart from God's divine purpose for their lives.

Purpose is what drives us to attempt things that are bigger than we are. It makes destiny clear and life meaningful. Purpose is finding God's will for your life. The purpose God has designed you for is like a diamond that is prepaid, hand crafted, crystal clear and flawless. Yet, it may start out as a lump of coal—a diamond in the rough. Maybe you cannot see the diamond yet. Maybe those around you cannot see it, but God knows what the end will be. He knows what He has designed for you to become.

To determine what God's purpose is for you, I recommend that you follow the instructions of Psalm 37:4–5:

> Delight thyself also in the LORD; and he shall give thee desires of thine heart. Commit thy way unto the LORD; trust also in him; and he shall bring it to pass.

Consider the strongest desires you are aware of that you would consider a dream for your life. Look deeply within to the desire that is always there, the one that is never pushed out even when other desires come and go. Once you find it, make sure that it lines up with the Word of God. Consult your pastor and others whom you consider to be mature Christians, sharing with them your desires. They will be able to counsel you regarding how to fulfill those desires that God has given you.

PURPOSE MAKES DESTINY CLEAR AND LIFE MEANINGFUL.

Finding your divine purpose and destiny in God will not happen overnight; it will take time. But I believe you will find that as you pursue it, the inner conflict you suffered because of lack of purpose will subside; you will begin to enjoy the pursuit of that which can satisfy your heart—the divine destiny for which you were designed.

Keys to Overcoming Symptoms of Depression

After you determine to discover your divine destiny, you can also apply these keys to overcoming feelings of despondency. One of the most important things to consider is the *attitude* with which you approach life. Attitude is defined as a way of thinking or behaving. I once heard a statement regarding attitude that I think hits the nail on the head: *Your attitude determines your altitude.* I believe this is very true. When you evaluate your attitude and find that it is filled with ideas of defeat, you can be sure that you will not fly very high toward reaching your goals. The following chart can help you determine where your attitude needs adjusting in order to be an overcomer in life.

DETERMINE YOUR ATTITUDE

Overcomer Attitude	Defeated Attitude
Celebrates success and victory	Celebrates failure and defeat
Considers how far they have gone	Asks how far they have to go
Rejoices in doing what it takes	Complains about why it takes so long
Encourages others	Demands that others encourage them
Receives their joy from the Lord	Steals the joy from other people
Takes responsibility for their mistakes	Blames others for their mistakes
Finds ways to correct problems	Presents problems that are always someone else's fault

It is a fact of life that some people approach the most difficult situations with an overcomer mentality, determined to do what it takes to celebrate success. Others approach situations in life with negative outlooks, complaining about how hard life is and expecting others to make them feel better. Some people choose to be optimistic; others walk in pessimism. Life offers you daily choices to decide whether you will celebrate success or failure, victory or defeat. Celebrating success means you choose positive expressions of laughter, praise, rejoicing, even dancing and clapping your hands. These are all expressions of celebrating victory. Celebrating defeat will be expressed by moaning, groaning, whining, complaining, wailing, slouching, hanging your head and even avoiding church functions. These are all expressions of "celebrating" defeat.

Did you locate yourself in the chart above? Most of us can use an attitude adjustment at particular times in our life. The Scriptures are filled with instructions regarding how we should learn to think and act to be overcomers in life. Proverbs 4:23–27 declares:

Keep thy heart with all diligence; for out of it are the issues of life. Put away from thee a froward mouth, and perverse lips put far from thee. Let thine eyes look right on, and let thine eyelids look straight before thee. Ponder the path of thy feet, and let all thy ways be established. Turn not to the right hand nor to the left: remove thy foot from evil.

To summarize, if your heart is right, you will think right, talk right and walk right. If you want to maintain a godly attitude, maintain a check on your heart. The writer of Proverbs also declared, "As he [a man] thinketh in his heart, so is he" (Prov. 23:7). Attitude does not just involve our mental outlook; it is also reflected in our goals and actions, and it influences whom we become.

Another key to overcoming symptoms of depression, once you have adjusted your attitude, is to set practical goals for your life according to your understanding of your purpose, which we discussed earlier. A goal may be simply defined as

> **LIFE OFFERS YOU DAILY CHOICES TO DECIDE WHETHER YOU WILL CELEBRATE SUCCESS OR FAILURE, VICTORY OR DEFEAT.**

"an object toward which effort is directed." Every day of our lives we need to set short-term goals and work to achieve them. How often do you wake up thinking about all the things you need to do that day? Setting goals and making a plan to accomplish them will give you a sense of purpose for that day.

After these short-term goals come mid-range goals such as further education, financial increase and other goals that will take longer than a day. And we need to consider long-term goals such as retirement. Goals must be given conscious recognition or they will never be achieved. The secret to setting goals and achieving them is to write them down and monitor their completion. When you create a habit of monitoring your goals, you will be more likely to achieve them.

In summary, let me list five keys to life that I believe will help you immensely in dealing with symptoms of depression:

1. PURPOSE—finding God's will for your life
2. ATTITUDE—forming God's character in you
3. GOALS—making plans for what you want to accomplish in life
4. DESTINY—understanding what God expects of you
5. VISION—embracing the hope God gives for your future

Having addressed the lesser causes of symptoms of depression—suppression and oppression—let's discuss the issues involved in the true condition of clinical depression.

Clinical Depression

The medical definition of *depression* is "a mental state of depressed mood characterized by feelings of sadness, despair and discouragement."[4] Generally, people who suffer with this condition have very low morale and low self-esteem. They suffer from loss of ambition and a giving-up, victim attitude. These mental symptoms are usually accompanied by a variety of physical symptoms that include fatigue, malaise, unexplained crying spells, unreasonable sadness, pain and generalized poor health status. Some cases also experience dark thoughts and morbid thinking, which can include suicidal thoughts.

With all of these symptoms, both mental and physical, it is important to separate issues and define the causes. True clinical depression from a causative standpoint can be a result of severe hormone imbalances, brain damage (such as from trauma, chemicals or drugs), brain pathology (brain lesions), neurotransmitter and ganglionic malfunctions, from severe grief; it can run the gamut from a personal crisis to loss of a loved one. These depressive "events" should be treated as medical emergencies, especially if someone has mentioned thoughts of killing someone else or themselves. These patients need to be stabilized and medically managed with medications. Once they have received stabilization care, the addition of natural medicine may be beneficial.

It is also important that patients suffering clinical depression receive spiritual help. Reading comforting passages of Scripture (such as Psalm 23 or Psalm 91) can help to bring peace to a troubled mind and heart. Having a friend or pastor pray with them can also be very helpful. Even when life does its worst to us, God has promised to be a present help in our deepest trouble (Ps. 46:1).

The fact is, however, that only a small percentage of patients actually suffer from true clinical depression. Most people with symptoms of depression fall into the categories we have discussed of suppression of the body or oppression of the mind. It is unfortunate that the medical community fails to note these causes of depression and treats symptoms of depression with drugs and medications instead. As Christians, it is imperative that we make a clear distinction between these conditions—suppression, oppression and clinical depression. Otherwise, you may find yourself medicated for symptoms of depression without ever addressing the root cause of the condition. When that happens, you can never expect a permanent cure.

Prozac, Zoloft, Paxil and others like them are being prescribed by thousands of physicians on a regular basis for patients who complain of symptoms of depression. I think people are being overmedicated in this area. I recommend that you sort out the issues we have discussed here regarding physical suppression and mental and emotional oppression, applying the protocols presented here before considering medicating with prescribed drugs. As I have said, unless you

> ONLY A SMALL PERCENTAGE OF PATIENTS ACTUALLY SUFFER FROM TRUE CLINICAL DEPRESSION.

feel you have severe symptoms of true clinical depression, you do have other options for treatment that will eliminate the cause instead of simply treating the symptom. However, if you suspect clinical depression, then by all means, seek a healthcare professional immediately before your condition causes you or anyone else any harm.

Recognizing the SAD syndrome

Keep in mind that some people start to feel depressed in the fall and winter months, especially on dark or dreary days. This condition is called *seasonal affective disorder* (SAD). This condition mimics depression but responds very well to natural, corrective measures.

Here are a few ways to combat the SAD syndrome:

- Open all of the blinds and curtains in your house to allow maximum entrance of light available.

- Take walks outdoors, especially during the morning hours. Exercise regularly.

- Spend as much time as possible outdoors or at least around windows so you can see outside.

- Turn on as many lights in your house as you can to provide a cheerful atmosphere indoors.

- If you live in an area with a particularly gloomy winter climate, there are special lights you can buy that will simulate sunlight for your brain, which can be very helpful during those dark months.

If you find yourself going to the doctor about the same time every fall or winter because you just feel bad all over, you may be experiencing symptoms of SAD. Following some of these suggestions should certainly make you feel much better.

Of course, you also need to consider hormonal imbalance as a possible cause for feelings of depression, as we discussed in chapter seven. By seriously evaluating these causes for symptoms of depression, you may find that relatively simple lifestyle changes can eliminate them altogether in a relatively short time. Giving the body proper nutrients and supplements along with exercise and adequate light, honestly evaluating your possible need to forgive another and getting proper evaluation of hormone levels can bring a cure to your condition without resorting to prescribed drugs.

Let me leave you with one important note. If you are suffering with any of these symptoms, please do not give in to feelings of condemnation or thoughts that you must be spiritually weak. The conditions we have just discussed can afflict the strongest Christians at some point in their lives. They are real health challenges that need to be dealt with just as you would remove a splinter from your finger. Though that splinter does not signify spiritual weakness, it must be removed to promote health. So it is with symptoms of depression, regardless of the cause. My prayer is that you will be inspired to get to the root of the problem, eliminate the cause and move toward physical, mental and emotional health.

IMPLEMENTING THE DIVINE DESIGN

I beseech you therefore, brethren, by the mercies of God, that ye present your bodies a living sacrifice, holy, acceptable unto God, which is your reasonable service. And be not conformed to this world: but be ye transformed by the renewing of your mind, that ye may prove what is that good, and acceptable, and perfect, will of God.

—ROMANS 12:1–2

CHAPTER 10

Evaluating Your Belief System

It is a fact of life that we learn the majority of what we know about healthcare from a godless world system, much of which is motivated by profit. We have unconsciously absorbed a worldly philosophy of caring for the body God gave to us. Billions of dollars of media advertising give us such unforgettable phrases such as, "Plop, plop, fizz, fizz, oh _____." (Can you fill in the blank? I am sure you can.) And New Age and other ungodly philosophies have clouded the picture with their systems of healing as well.

Before I continue to help you evaluate your belief system regarding healthcare and God's design for your body, let me once again say that I am not against the medical profession or medical science. I believe there are many sincere and skilled physicians whose goal is to increase their patients' quality of health. What I am going to highlight, however, is what I believe is a flawed system, which we need to consider when we choose our approach to healthcare.

Symptomatic Approach

The typical philosophy for medical treatment focuses on finding relief for symptoms, not a cure for the cause of the symptoms. That is why over-the-counter medications are such big business. Even prescription drugs often treat only pain or inflammation, without being able to effect true healing of the disease. We are taught from the time we are small children that if we get sick or if something hurts, we need to take something for relief. Hence, another household line: "How do you spell relief? R-O-L-A-I-D-S." The sad truth is that when we get sick, too often we do not look for a cure that is available to us in God's design; instead we look for relief from the symptoms.

We have been educated to consider *primary* healthcare to function like the following scenario. A patient gets sick and goes to the doctor. The doctor examines the patient and makes a diagnosis. He then recommends a prescription medication that is produced by a pharmaceutical company. The doctor may also make a prognosis, predicting the patient's long-term outcome. The patient is given a prescription, perhaps with an explanation in lay terms of what it will do for him or her. The patient then has the prescription filled, and he follows the instructions for taking it. This typical treatment protocol seems harmless; we have all done it.

However, our healthcare system is first of all based in a belief system. All belief systems promote a way of practice to be established in order to allow the participants to accomplish certain goals. Standards of practice are devised as rules to maintain the integrity of the belief system. It is this belief system that is flawed, even from its beginning centuries ago, which we need to evaluate carefully so that we do not relate to it unwisely. Let me share with you a few core beliefs of our current medical system that may surprise you.

A Flawed System

Beginning with Hippocrates, the Father of Medicine, who lived in the fifth and fourth centuries before Christ, we observe pagan origins and practices for physicians. So renowned is Hippocrates as the first healer to attempt to record medical experiences for future reference that today's physicians take an oath to practice medicine using his words. The oath begins:

I swear by Apollo the physician, by Aesculapius, and Hygeia,

and Panacea, and all the gods and goddesses, that according
to my ability and judgment, I will keep this oath and its stip-
ulation—to reckon him who taught me this art equally dear
to me as my parents…[1]

It is significant to note the gods to which this medical belief
system swears allegiance. Aesculapius is the ancient Greek god of
medicine, whose symbol in modern medicine is a staff with a snake
wrapped around it.[2] While this fact does not obviously corrupt all
the good that medical science can accomplish today, I believe we
need to consider the source of our belief systems as Christians and
be cautious regarding where they lead.

In the ancient world a physician was a magician or pagan priest
who performed primitive medical practices.[3] Their treatments were
largely unscientific and mythical. Hippocrates separated physical
causes for disease from magical or mythical relationships. This was
a great step of progress for the organized practice of medicine,
which he established, bringing clear separation between science and
mysticism.

The problem that stems from that approach is that medical science began to separate the physical and spiritual aspects of
humanity to a fault. Medical science has become agnostic and atheistic in its approach to curing human ills. From that point, healing
for disease and illness has focused strictly on the physical aspects,
disregarding man as a spiritual being.

Given these considerations, we need to examine our allegiance to
a medical system that does not acknowledge God's design for
healing and health. If we place our faith in a godless system, we will
find it difficult to have faith for God's promises to heal. The reason
most believers aren't able to walk into the health benefits that are
promised in the Word of God is because they don't position themselves to receive that liberty. The apostle Paul discussed the
believers' position of liberty in his letter to the Galatians: "Stand fast
therefore in the liberty wherewith Christ hath made us free, and be
not entangled again with the yoke of bondage" (Gal. 5:1).

The liberty of the believer is dependent, according to the

Scriptures, on his walking in the Spirit and obeying the law of God. If we violate the principles God has given us regarding taking responsibility for the care of our body, we will jeopardize our freedom. Jesus died for our healing, and we can receive that promise as we position ourselves to live in His grace. The apostle Paul declared that if we do the works of the flesh, which include "adultery, fornication, uncleanness, lasciviousness, idolatry, witchcraft, hatred, variance, emulations, wrath, strife, seditions, heresies, envyings, murders, drunkenness, revellings, and such like," we cannot inherit the kingdom of God (Gal. 5:19–21).

In today's society many of the above list are accepted as a normal lifestyle, even though they have spawned many new diseases as a result. We need to base our belief system for healthcare on biblical principles that will assure a healthy lifestyle and give us the promises of abundant life in the kingdom: "righteousness, and peace, and joy in the Holy Ghost" (Rom. 14:17).

We need to examine medical treatments as to whether they promote life and health or simply treat symptoms of a disease, thus deceiving us into accepting a godless solution that will not cure our ill. It is interesting, for example, that the Greek word from which we derive pharmaceuticals (prescription drugs) is *pharmakeia*, which is translated in Scripture as *witchcraft* (Gal. 5:20).[4] It contains the meanings of a drug or spell-giving potion as well as a poisoner. Spells and incantations were used both to restore health and to destroy enemies.

At the risk of being thought extreme, I want to caution you not to simply accept drugs as medications, which are foreign to the body and often cause side effects. The approach to healing I have discussed with you in these pages will address the root cause of illness as well as areas of disobedience to the Word of God if you are not properly caring for your body. Again, I understand that there are times when prescription medications or even over-the-counter products may be necessary. But it is important that you consider where you are placing your confidence and trust for healing, and that you learn to take responsibility to walk in God's ways to gain true freedom from illness and disease.

On the Flip Side

While I choose to think of the natural approach to healing as *primary* healthcare, which is supported by biblical principles that instruct us to take responsibility for our bodies, I understand that from the perspective of medical science, the natural approach is referred to as alternative medicine. Unfortunately, that category of healing is also flawed; just because *alternative medicine* is used does not automatically mean it is safe.

The public has been encouraged to "try alternative medicine to avoid the side effects of drugs." Although in many cases this is legitimate, it is also a fact that some herbal treatments produce side effects like many of the chemical drugs now being used. It is even a fact that many pharmaceutical drugs used today have an herbal origin. While herbs are usually safer than prescription drugs, a person must use caution in taking them to avoid the possibility of side effects also. For example, some herbal products work as natural diuretics, but if they are consumed too often or in high doses, they can produce dehydration.

Once again, we need to be aware of the philosophy behind the ones who are promoting and practicing any "natural" approach to healing. Metaphysicists, psychics and spiritists all practice "medicine" often using natural substances. However, their anti-Christ origins can be traced back into history beyond the days of Moses. Their practices still attempt to mock the true power of the living God, defying His divine design to heal the body, mind and spirit.

In Summary

The reason I have felt it necessary to help you evaluate your belief system regarding your medical care is because most people place their faith in our current medical system. And I have cautioned you regarding alternative medicine because I believe it is also a flawed system, as I have discussed.

However, I do not want to overlook the contributions of either healing system to the good and healing of their patients. I am well aware that all diagnosis-prognosis reports do not attempt to fill patients with fear. Most have positive outcomes with successful results. There are good, moral medical doctors who are attempting to treat their patients in a caring and proper manner. I also understand that all medicines do not qualify as *pharmakeia* (poison).

I am only concerned that too often faith is being placed entirely on the report of a doctor or a medical examination. Please determine to be open-minded, and consider evaluating any recommended treatment, whether medical or alternative. And let me share with you another wonderful provision of God's *healing by design:* divine healing.

CHAPTER 11

Faith and Divine Healing

Picture this: You are sitting in a waiting room of a hospital. You are starting to get restless because one of your loved ones is being examined for something that could prove to be serious. The tension mounts as the smell of alcohol and antiseptics provide a familiar aroma associated with memories of past traumas. The doctors and nurses in their white coats briskly rush through the hallways communicating in what seems almost a foreign language. The longer you wait, the harder your heart starts to pound as you begin imagining all of the possible scenarios the doctor's report may bring. After hours of waiting, fear begins to set in and to take control of your senses.

The anxiety builds as you watch the double doors with the small windows, hoping for a glimpse of your loved one. *Is he OK? Is it serious? Can it be treated?* Your entire focus is centered on waiting for the doctor to make his grand entrance. Finally, with your adrenaline flowing, palms sweating and your heart racing, you try to maintain your composure as the doctor slowly moves toward you. The entire time he talks with you, he continues staring down at the results on his clipboard and tapping his pen.

Sound familiar? Most of us have lived through a similar experience.

The Arena of Fear

What amazes me about this hypothetical situation is that no matter how much you have prayed and confessed your faith in God to heal, fear still sneaks in. I personally have witnessed this phenomenon many times in my life. I call it the *arena of fear*. I am concerned that some doctors manipulate patients and family members through fear to get them to agree to expensive procedures that may not be necessary. Do you suppose it really has to be this way? Or is there a better way?

I have seen people taken advantage of because they did not know "what the doctor knew." I am convinced that unnecessary aggressive procedures have been performed as a result of the patient's fear after placing his or her confidence in a professional who was not above being motivated by profit. Often patients are expected to make healthcare decisions in a moment that will affect them for a lifetime. Instead of taking the time to become informed and considering the options they have for treatment, they are given an ultimatum regarding the potential life-threatening situation they are facing.

Fear will make people come to decisions that they would not otherwise consider. If fear is the motivating factor, they may agree to take harmful chemicals, sacrifice limbs or follow a multitude of radical procedures. Chemotherapy and radiation are examples of potentially harmful treatments for which I believe these scare tactics are sometimes employed. And we must consider the possibility of a profit motive, considering that a single treatment may cost between twenty and thirty thousand dollars.

The best advice I can offer you is to never make a health decision based on fear. Fear is the opposite of faith. Though fear is often a reaction to the unknown, it is not a part of the original design.

A Faith Response

The Word of God declares:

> For God hath not given us the spirit of fear; but of power, and of love, and of a sound mind.
>
> —2 TIMOTHY 1:7

The "sound mind" described in this verse could also be translated as a disciplined mind. Disciplining our thoughts to consider the truths of God's Word and following His principles for health will be a strong deterrent to the spirit of fear that would attack us from all sides. Isn't this a strong picture of God's design for our health— power, love and a sound mind? It is

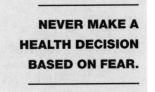

NEVER MAKE A HEALTH DECISION BASED ON FEAR.

worth putting our faith in a loving God who offers such wonderful benefits. Where is your faith? Perhaps to begin our discussion of how we can receive divine healing by faith, we should consider an even more basic question: What is faith?

Faith 101

The *Oxford American Dictionary* defines *faith* simply as "reliance or trust in a person or thing."[1] If you have no faith in yourself, you will not succeed in your goals. If you have no faith in your spouse, you cannot expect to enjoy a good marriage. Faith is a reality that reflects our core beliefs. Someone who is facing surgery places his or her faith in the surgeon. If the patient did not have faith in the surgeon, he would not submit to the procedure. What we do or don't do depends on where we place our faith.

Scripture declares, "Now faith is the substance of things hoped for, the evidence of things not seen" (Heb. 11:1). When we read that verse, we often tend to focus on "things hoped for" and "things not seen." That leaves faith in a nebulous, vague arena, which is a sign of weak faith! Why? Because it leaves out God's guarantee for "substance" and "evidence." Things that are hoped for and things not seen belong to the realm of the imagination; they are intangible. But "substance" and "evidence" are tangible; therefore, they are obtainable. Receiving God's guarantee of substance and evidence is what produces strong faith. It is very important that you develop a strong faith that states its purpose based on the guarantees of the Word of God.

Unless we understand what faith is, we may think we have faith without experiencing the reality of it. For example, here are four "kinds" of faith:

1. *Religious faith* says, "Lord, I know You can help me today." It rests in the knowledge of God's ability, without believing His willingness to do it.

2. *Weak faith* says, "Lord, if it is Your will, please help me." It rests in faulty knowledge or lack of knowledge of the Word of God, hence not knowing the will of God—His desire—to help.

3. *No faith* says, "I cannot be helped." This attitude of unbelief needs to be repented of so that you can experience the "measure of faith" God gives to everyone (Rom. 12:3).

4. *Strong faith* says, "I can do all things through Christ which strengtheneth me" (Phil. 4:13).

Where do you see yourself in this list? I can honestly tell you that if you picked any one of those choices except number four, you need to make some honest changes in your approach to God. Strong faith only sees what God has spoken. It has no other option. F. F. Bosworth stated, "If your faith is saying anything other than what God's Word declares, you are only walking in mental reasoning, which is hostile to God (Rom. 8:7)."[2] Hebrews 11:6 says, "But without faith it is impossible to please him: for he that cometh to God must believe that he is, and that he is a rewarder of them that diligently seek him."

In order to receive divine healing, you have to know who God is and diligently seek Him as the loving Father who promises healing and health. The real question that needs to be asked is, Who is your healer? If I asked you right now, what would your answer be? F. F. Bosworth also remarked in his book *Christ the Healer* regarding faith:

> The fact is, that the very first covenant that God gave after the passage of the Red Sea, which was so distinctively typical of our redemption, was the covenant of healing, and it was

at this time that God revealed himself as our physician, by the first redemptive and covenant name, Jehova-Rapha, I am the Lord that healeth thee. This is not only a promise, it is a statute or ordinance and so, corresponding to this ancient ordinance, we have, in the command of James 5:14, a positive ordinance of healing in Christ's name as sacred and binding upon every church today as the ordinances of the Lord's supper and of the Christian baptism.[3]

Once again the promise is not the problem; the problem is the lack of willingness of people to accept it. Salvation is hard for some people to accept because it seems too good to be true that we can be forgiven of all our sins and have an eternal relationship with God. However, when a person makes a commitment to Christ in faith, real changes begin to take place in their lives. A wonderful sense of freedom from guilt and a joy of heart begin to be felt by new believers. Though all circumstances of life, especially those that are consequences of sinful behavior, may not end at once, the joy of sins forgiven helps our faith to grow in the Lord.

Sometimes it takes years to see God's plan fully unfold in people's lives. Yet, if they remain faithful and adhere to His Word, they will eventually prosper in every area. When it comes to healing, these same principles apply. The health condition may not turn around right away, but as you place your faith in God for healing, He will be faithful to heal you. It may take some time before you experience complete healing. You may have to demonstrate your faith in the design of your Creator and in the inherent recuperative powers that He placed inside every created being.

Consider how divine healing comes to us. Healing power flows from above (from God), then down to earth (through Jesus), then inside you (by the Holy Spirit) and then outward—in power of life for you and others. Scriptures declare of Jesus that "God anointed Jesus of Nazareth with the Holy Ghost and with power: who went about doing good, and healing all that were oppressed of the devil; for God was with him" (Acts 10:38). This divine flow of life is what God has promised to the true believer. This is His covenant of healing that is available to them that believe.

If you understand and believe this concept of healing, the only thing that can separate you from your healing is to allow yourself to be distracted from the teachings in the Word, which instruct you how to walk in God to live in health. Anything that interferes with that divine communication, which connects you to the Spirit of God, cuts off the life's source that feeds the spirit. It is important to understand that life proceeds from the spirit, not the body. It is the spirit that is in charge of the body, not the body that is in charge of the spirit.

Following wrong principles, wrong beliefs and wrong practices can block the perfect flow of life from God's Spirit to your spirit, interrupting the balance of mind and body that it needs for health. God's Word is His promise. Just as He fulfilled the Creation plan and the human design, so He fulfills His Word to us as well. The problem of not receiving divine healing, once again, does not begin with God; it lies in His people. Too often believers want to have the promises of God work for them without separating themselves from the destructive ways of the world. The world, with all of its enticements, continually holds men captive on a course headed for destruction. Unless a man chooses life through the renewing of the mind by the Word of God, as Paul wrote in Romans 12:1–2, he will suffer the consequences of self-destruction. The writer of Proverbs declared:

> My son, attend to my words; incline thine ear unto my say-
> ings. Let them not depart from thine eyes; keep them in the
> midst of thine heart. For they are life unto those that find
> them, and health to all their flesh.
>
> —PROVERBS 4:20–22

Why don't you give some of the principles for health you have read in this book a chance? You may have already tried everything else. Why not try something based on absolute truth—the Bible? As I mentioned, this is just a brief synopsis of faith for divine healing and the promises of God concerning it. They are a necessary foundation to begin your search for faith that can change your life and impact your health. It ultimately comes down to the question of where you are willing to place your faith. If you do not expect to receive the Bible's promises of life and healing, it will not seem important that you obey the Word of God. However, if you want to receive the promises of healing, you will have to be willing to seek God's way and make some changes in your lifestyle.

CHAPTER 12

Your Reasonable Service

I have wondered why people receive helpful information about healing and health and still do not make any changes in their lifestyle. The information is clear. It is based on principles from the Word of God, and yet they still choose not to follow them. How many times I have personally witnessed this sad reality with my patients, friends and even family members.

I think part of the answer for their response (or lack of it) is a false sense of security. They reason, "That will not happen to me," or they procrastinate, "I'm going to start next week." The list of excuses or reasonings goes on and on. The problem with excuses is that they only build a false sense of security, which amounts to a lie.

Putting off the things that will improve your health could cost you your life. Excuses are a form of setting goals that temporarily soothe your conscience without making any lasting change. Without change, the internal problems of your body continue to worsen. I believe that your reading this book is not a coincidence; it is proof that God loves you. He is reaching out to you with knowledge that can lead you to a healthier way of life.

Just recently I received the news that a young man in his thirties was in the hospital because of a heart attack. Sadly, this young man had come into my clinic two years earlier for a health consultation.

He was given counsel and health recommendations, which I believe could have prevented the eventual heart attack. He also attended several health lectures that I present weekly. He had more than enough information and resources to initiate the necessary changes his body needed for improved health. But as so many people do, he continued to put it off for one more day.

The good news is that he survived his heart attack and will get another chance to pursue a healthy lifestyle. The bad news is that it took a trip to the hospital and a near-death experience to get him to change his lifestyle. If he had only listened to the recommendations provided to him two years earlier, it is quite possible he could have been spared that trauma. Other people had also encouraged him to make healthy lifestyle changes, but he made excuses for his procrastination. When he was admitted to the hospital, the physicians had to place him on Coumadin (warfarin), which has the same chemical composition as rat poison. The crisis situation of a heart attack demanded that treatment in order to save his life. Now, not only does he have to make lifestyle changes, but he has to take rat poison as well. What a shame.

So many times patients come through my clinic and do not follow the recommendations given them. Others read information like the information you are reading in this book. Yet they still refuse to make any changes. I think about the thousands of diabetics who refuse to quit drinking alcohol or eating sugar and refined carbohydrates even when they know it is killing them. I personally know of many diabetics who have lost toes, feet and legs and have developed other extreme health conditions as a result of being rebellious and unwilling to change. The Bible clearly states our responsibility to cooperate with divine laws:

> I beseech you therefore, brethren, by the mercies of God, that ye present your bodies a living sacrifice, holy, acceptable unto God, which is your reasonable service.
>
> —ROMANS 12:1

For our bodies to be holy and acceptable to the Lord, we need to consider that we care for them as we would any other valuable possession. In 2 Corinthians 6:16, the apostle Paul also calls our body a temple of the living God, making it a reverent place of great value.

I believe that if we are to fulfill our responsibility for keeping our bodies healthy, we will have to understand the following verse: "And be not conformed to this world: but be ye transformed by the renewing of your mind, that ye may prove what is that good, and acceptable, and perfect, will of God" (Rom. 12:2). Conforming to the world's standards for eating will likely make you a part of our carboholic society and expose you to the risk of the top three killer diseases, as we have discussed. The world's system of eating is creating life-threatening conditions for young and old alike.

In order for you to enjoy health, you must take responsibility to place back into your system the nutrients that your body needs to stay alive. Good health will require you to cleanse the chemicals and pollution from your system so they do not cause damage that leads to sickness and disease. It will involve using natural substances that God created in Genesis 1:29 to accomplish this cleansing without suffering harmful side effects.

Have you heard of *essential* vitamins, minerals, amino acids and fatty acids? Do you know why they are called "essential"? Simply because you have to have them to live. They are essential—necessary—to life. They are not optional; they must be consumed in order to sustain life. As a matter of fact, if your system becomes deficient in any of these substances your body will begin displaying symptoms much like a car spitting, sputtering or lurching when it is low on fuel. The body has a set of symptoms that it will manifest if it is low on these nutrients. Part of our reasonable service in consecrating our bodies to God is to take responsibility for giving them proper nutrients for health.

This past week I was watching a fishing program about a man whose boat was capsized during a sudden storm. The waves began to roll into the boat, and in a matter of moments his boat was filled with water and he found himself swimming with waves splashing against the sides of his body and continually pushing him under. To hear him tell it, it was quite a struggle. What touched me the most was the comment he made about his thoughts during that crisis. He said, "When I was floating in the water, all I could think about was that I wished that I had time to scratch a message down for my wife and family." It amazed me because he was not consumed with the fear of the situation, nor was his mind preoccupied with planning his escape. Instead he was thinking about the effect his demise would have on his loved ones.

Sickness can affect our lives suddenly, much like that fisherman's accident. It can rob us of our destinies and profoundly impact our families. If you fail to maintain your body properly, giving it the substances it needs to stay alive, or if you put harmful things into your body, you are heading toward a tragedy. Many people who live irresponsibly in this way do not get another chance to make the corrections or to say good-bye to loved ones.

You only receive one body for your entire lifetime. If you only had one house, one car and one set of clothes in this lifetime, how would you maintain them? What kind of care would you offer them to ensure longevity and durability? The sad truth is that often we spend more on our cars, homes and clothes than we do on taking care of the body that God has given us. Of course, we spend thousands of dollars on medical bills once we have become ill. It would seem more reasonable to spend some of those dollars on maintenance to avoid the high cost of illness.

Rather than spending your money on remedies from drugs to surgery to all kinds of expensive treatments, I recommend that you spend some money on preventative measures, like vitamins and minerals. Pharmaceutical companies certainly stand to lose the most in a vitamin/mineral war. As major contributors offering financial support to medical institutions that train the doctors, their influence is felt. If a patient can correct deficiencies and eliminate symptoms by simply adding vitamins and minerals back into their diet, the pharmaceutical companies could lose business. I know many physicians who still think vitamin supplementation is a gimmick because of what they were taught in medical school. However, the truth still remains that the body can rebuild itself when given proper nutrients.

A Final Thought

I've often wondered why the practice of replacing nutrients that the body must have in order to live and function, as well as using herbal preparations (God's provision) that naturally cleanse the body's filtration systems, is called *alternative medicine!* It is my conviction that natural medicine as we have discussed in this book should be considered primary healthcare. I would then consider it more accurate to refer to conventional medicine as emergency healthcare and surgery, as a last resort, as extensive healthcare.

No matter what you call it, however, the maintenance of the body is our primary responsibility in order to assure healing and health. We cannot expect a doctor to heal us; that is an impossibility. If we understand the divine design of our bodies, we will know why we must dedicate our lives to walking in health principles that God has made clear in His Word. Fulfilling His will, encountering our destiny and enjoying the longevity God promises depend on our accepting the truth of *Healing by Design.*

CHAPTER 13

Designed As a
Peculiar People

As physicians, we are not responsible for the outcome of someone's sickness; we are only responsible for the methods we use to inspire healing. This is similar to when we witness to a person about Jesus Christ; we are responsible to give them correct information based on the Word of God, but we are not responsible for the outcome of whether they receive salvation or not. Our intent must be to bring healing. But intent alone, no matter how noble or good, cannot bring healing. Good intentions can be misdirected by faulty information or an incorrect approach to healing that is not biblical.

Because a physician is a Christian with noble intentions to bring healing to his or her patients, it does not necessarily follow that his methods or approach to healing is in line with Bible teaching. Although his motives may be pure, that alone does not assure that he can bring healing to the body based on his clinical training. As a Christian, I have had to make many hard decisions regarding my approach to practicing as a physician. Anyone who decides to do things differently from what much of society considers the "norm" risks being considered weird or peculiar.

For example, as you have read this book, you have learned that attacking every disease symptom with a different pill or drug is not necessarily the prescription for finding a cure; it only alleviates certain symptoms while often causing other side effects. And we have discussed the fact that many people are sick simply because they have nutrient deficiencies, chemical toxicities and clogged filters. They eat dead refined foods, most of which are converted in the body into the drug called "sugar." As a result, they spend much of their lives combating symptoms with "relief medications," which are chemicals that produce massive amounts of cell damage (side effects). They are stressed out to the max and use other chemical vices to alleviate their stress. Unfortunately, this description is a typical scenario of the average day in the life of a "normal" American—even Christians.

In many places the Bible refers to God's people as a peculiar people (1 Pet. 2:9; Titus 2:14; Ps. 135:4). For example, the Lord declared to Israel:

> The LORD hath chosen thee to be a peculiar people unto
> himself, above all the nations that are upon the earth.
> —DEUTERONOMY 14:2

Contained in the meaning of "peculiar" are the beautiful concepts of a purchased possession, special, proper, good and separated unto God.[1] It does not mean "strange" or "eccentric," as today's usage has evolved to imply. As God's peculiar people, we should be willing to conform to His requirements for the divine design that He initiated for our good. What is truly amazing to me is that when you practice the recommendations based on your divine design, and adhere to them strictly and without compromise, many people, including Christians, think you are "strange" or "eccentric."

We should not relegate our responsibility for maintaining the divine design of our bodies completely to medical doctors. Too many Christians have placed their total health care in the hands of an overworked, under-managed healthcare system. The doctors are working hard to do their jobs well; the problem is that we need to be taking our proper responsibility. If we would manage our body the way people manage successful businesses (with schedules, goal setting, diligent planning), the condition of healthcare in this nation could change drastically.

Good health is not achieved by luck, chance, genetics or even mental awareness. Instead, it is the result of a lifestyle of good habits and solid health practices that make sense. Sometimes it is hard to believe that such a dramatic change can take place in the restoration of one's health just by making a few practical lifestyle changes. It all boils down to making right choices along with the discipline to carry them out.

Last Call

Today is the beginning of the rest of your life. Why not start out on the right foot? How much value do you place on your life? How badly do you desire excellent health? As you finish reading this book, I challenge you to decide to make changes right now. Take the health survey and follow the appropriate protocol for you. Consider the need for supplementation based on the fact that foods grown in our depleted soils are deficient and that toxins need to be removed from your body every day. This means your body requires supplementation and cleansing.

Determine to be consistent. You owe it to your body. Remember, some people never get a second chance to make a change. Try to recover from your bad habits and from the way the "fast food" world has trained you to take care of your body. Continually do things to improve the quality of your nervous system, such as exercise, stretching and chiropractic adjustments. This will promote better communication throughout the system. You can still make a difference for yourself and for those who love and care about you. To help you grasp the enormous power you have in making choices, I want to leave you with this one last call in the words of a challenging little poem by an unknown author called simply, *Recovery*.

Recovery

There are five short chapters in the book of recovery:

CHAPTER 1
I walk down the street.
There is a deep hole in the sidewalk.
I fall in.
I am lost. I am hopeless!!!
It is not my fault!!

CHAPTER 2
I walk down the same street.
There is a deep hole in the sidewalk.
I pretend I do not see it.
I fall in again.
I cannot believe I am in the same place.
But it is not my fault.
It still takes a long time to get out.

CHAPTER 3
I walk down the same street.
There is a deep hole in the sidewalk.
I see it is there.
I still fall in. It is a habit.
My eyes are open.
I know where I am.
It is my fault.
I get out immediately.

CHAPTER 4
I walk down the same street.
There is a deep hole in the sidewalk.
I walk around it.

CHAPTER 5
I walk down another street.

—AUTHOR UNKNOWN

HEALTH PROTOCOLS AND DIETS

He causeth the grass to grow for the cattle, and herb for the service of man: that he may bring forth food out of the earth; and wine that maketh glad the heart of man, and oil to make his face to shine, and bread which strengtheneth man's heart.

—PSALM 104:14–15

CHAPTER 14

Life Support System Health Survey

The following instructions will help you in filling out the Life Support System Health Survey and determining which protocol you should follow:

- Place a check in the boxes of those symptoms you experience on a regular or semi-regular basis.

- Next, count up each of the checks in the subgroups listed in each category and place the total in the boxes provided next to the number of the subgroup (such as B-1, B-2, B-3).

- Next, tally up the small boxes in each section by adding them together and placing the sum total of each category in the boxes provided next to the protocol letter (A, B, C or D).

- The category for which you have the highest number of marks is what you need to address first. For example, if category B has more checks than A, C or D, and B-2 has the most checks in that category, you should begin improving your health by following Protocol B-2. (See page 170.)

■ You should have four or more symptoms in one category in order to suggest the need of treatment.
Follow that protocol as accurately as possible for
four weeks; then retake the survey. Consider where
your symptoms have improved and where they may
need to be addressed at that point.

LIFE SUPPORT SYSTEM HEALTH SURVEY

A ❑

- ❑ Night blindness
- ❑ Dry eyes
- ❑ Sleep disturbances with bone pain associated
- ❑ Frequent fractures
- ❑ History of cystic fibrosis
- ❑ Chronic pancreatitis
- ❑ History of obstructive liver disease
- ❑ Excessive thirst
- ❑ Anxiety
- ❑ Trouble getting deep breath
- ❑ Outside of nostrils, external ear or eyelids become reddened, scaly, greasy, painful
- ❑ Painful fissures in center of mouth
- ❑ Painful tongue
- ❑ Scaling of skin
- ❑ Swollen, bright red tongue
- ❑ Depression with insomnia
- ❑ Wrist pain worse at night (or carpal tunnel syndrome)
- ❑ Numbness in extremities
- ❑ Irritable and depressed (both)
- ❑ Skin on face is dry, shining, scaling
- ❑ Inside of mouth and tongue sore
- ❑ Prolonged use of egg white protein supplement
- ❑ Hair loss
- ❑ Weight loss, indigestion, episodes of diarrhea (all present)
- ❑ Premature gray hair
- ❑ Mild jaundice
- ❑ History of cleft deformities
- ❑ Birth defects
- ❑ Feeling fatigued from stress
- ❑ Burning feet syndrome
- ❑ Faint feeling upon standing up quickly
- ❑ Chronic colds or being "sickly"
- ❑ Slow wound healing
- ❑ Leg cramps
- ❑ Frequent urination
- ❑ Taking diuretics
- ❑ Excessive sweating due to occupation or other causes
- ❑ Muscle spasms or fasciculations (involuntary twitches or contractions)

❏ Tremor
❏ Taking high amounts of calcium
❏ Rough, dry skin
❏ Swollen prostate (slowed urine flow)
❏ Lack of taste (cannot taste food well)
❏ Symptoms of unexplained chest pain
❏ White fingernail beds
❏ Chronic muscle pain and tenderness
❏ Blood sugar imbalance
❏ Lack of endurance
❏ Eat mostly carbohydrates

LIFE SUPPORT SYSTEM HEALTH SURVEY

B ❏

1 ❏
- ❏ Heavy alcohol use
- ❏ Sensitive to chemical smells (perfume, new car, pet, etc.)
- ❏ Sick headaches
- ❏ Natural or synthetic steroid use (anabolic steroids, estrogens or contraceptives)
- ❏ Unexplained heart symptoms (arrhythmia, rapid heartbeat, heart pounding)
- ❏ Depression
- ❏ Headaches
- ❏ Mental confusion
- ❏ Numbness and tingling
- ❏ Respiratory tract allergies
- ❏ High exposure to certain chemicals (cleaning solvents, pesticides, antibiotics, diuretics, thyroid medicine, NSAIDS, i.e., ibuprofen, Tylenol, etc.)

2 ❏
- ❏ Fatigue (unusual)
- ❏ Muscle pains (fairly constant)
- ❏ Symptoms worse after dental work
- ❏ Tremors
- ❏ Weakness in arms or legs
- ❏ Anemic
- ❏ Dizziness
- ❏ Poor coordination

3 ❏
- ❏ Migraine headaches
- ❏ Eczema
- ❏ Arthritis
- ❏ Inflamed bowel
- ❏ Asthma symptoms
- ❏ Irritable bowel
- ❏ Sinus congestion
- ❏ Indigestion
- ❏ Intestinal gas
- ❏ Diarrhea/constipation
- ❏ General fatigue
- ❏ Feeling worse after eating
- ❏ Rash or hives

LIFE SUPPORT SYSTEM HEALTH SURVEY

C ❑

   4 ❑
- ❑ Feel "spacey"
- ❑ Feel "drained"
- ❑ Spots in front of eyes
- ❑ Itching
- ❑ Symptoms worse on damp, muggy days
- ❑ Chronic infection of skin and nails
- ❑ Have taken antibiotics within last year
- ❑ Severely crave sugar, feel worse after eating it
- ❑ Chronic yeast infection

   5 ❑
- ❑ Abdominal cramps
- ❑ Rectal itching
- ❑ Flatulence and abdominal bloating
- ❑ Foul-smelling stools
- ❑ Abdominal distention
- ❑ Chronic low back pain
- ❑ Symptoms worse around full moon
- ❑ Eaten food out of the U.S. within past year
- ❑ Eat raw oysters or raw seafood
- ❑ Heartburn, nausea and vomiting (all three)

   6 ❑
- ❑ Night sweats
- ❑ Sore throat
- ❑ Swollen lymph glands
- ❑ Stomachache
- ❑ Cough
- ❑ Odd skin sensations
- ❑ Loss of appetite
- ❑ History of mononucleosis
- ❑ History of oral herpes, genital herpes or shingles
- ❑ History of Epstein-Barr virus (chronic fatigue syndrome)
- ❑ History of viral hepatitis

LIFE SUPPORT SYSTEM HEALTH SURVEY

D ☐

   7 ☐

- ☐ Eat mostly carbohydrate foods (rice, potatoes, pasta, bread, sweets, etc.)
- ☐ Eat or crave sweets (desserts, candy, etc.)
- ☐ Avoid eating meat
- ☐ Get shaky (or weak) if hungry
- ☐ Have lost weight using protein diets
- ☐ Have high cholesterol
- ☐ Eat junk food more than five times per week
- ☐ Eat fast food more than five times per week
- ☐ Drink sweetened beverages (sodas, sweet tea, Gatorade, juice, lemonade)
- ☐ Feel like you have to have something sweet with meal
- ☐ Are hypoglycemic or diabetic
- ☐ Presence of gallstones
- ☐ More than 20 pounds overweight

   8 ☐

- ☐ Exhaustion
- ☐ Low blood pressure
- ☐ Dry skin and hair
- ☐ Inappropriate weight gain
- ☐ Constipation
- ☐ High cholesterol
- ☐ Emotional, easily upset (cry for no reason)
- ☐ Have goiter
- ☐ Insomnia
- ☐ Feel cold when it is warm (or vice versa)
- ☐ Slow wound healing
- ☐ Panic attacks
- ☐ Cold hands or feet
- ☐ Light headed or ringing in ears
- ☐ Depression

In the next chapter you will find the protocols to follow to help improve your physical condition.

Health
Protocols

T he following protocols have proven very helpful when followed consistently. Start with the protocol developed for the area in which you showed the most responses in the health survey. Follow that protocol four to six weeks consistently until you see favorable results in the lessening of symptoms.

Sometimes the body will heal itself by removing layers of stresses in other areas when you follow a protocol for your most needed area. Continue to choose a different protocol where you have listed the most complaints, following each protocol for four to six weeks.

If you have only two or three symptoms in any category, you may be able to receive the help you need by just taking the *Primary Healthcare System* of supplements I have developed specifically for these health needs. If this is your choice, it is usually better to double your dosages for the first two weeks to saturate the system with nutrients and to provide an initial purge. Follow up with the maintenance dose each day as follows:

- *Protocols Life Support* taken at lunch
- *Protocols Incellate* taken at lunch
- *Protocols Tea Tox* taken at bedtime
- *Protocols Colon Therapy* taken at bedtime

167

Then consider adjusting your present nutritional regimen to include the *Stay Healthy Diet* on page 179.

AUTHOR'S NOTE: As stated earlier, this information is not intended to diagnose, treat or replace necessary medical care. I recommend that you consult your physician before taking any product or starting any diet.

Protocol A

This protocol is recommended for individuals who may have nutritional deficiencies that are causing unpleasant symptoms.

> **FOLLOW THE PROTOCOL OF YOUR CHOICE FOUR TO SIX WEEKS CONSISTENTLY.**

These deficiencies are usually created from chronic poor eating habits (for example, refined foods, fast food, junk food and packaged food). It's imperative that dietary changes are instituted, along with proper supplementation, in order to replenish the depleted system.

Also, because of the types of food that have been consumed, proper cleansing will be extremely beneficial. The supplement recommendations listed help the body manage both of these tasks (to replenish deficiencies and properly cleanse). Higher doses are recommended initially, followed by maintenance doses to prevent similar problems from recurring in the future.

Add to your nutritional regimen

- The *Stay Healthy Diet* (page 179)

- Vegetable and fruit juices (preferably try to buy organically grown fruits and vegetables and use a juicer)

- *Protocols Life Support:* Take two to three times daily with meals.

- *Protocols Incellate:* Take two to four capsules daily with meals.

- *Protocols Tea Tox and Protocols Colon Therapy:* Take one packet of each at bedtime (with 8 ounces of water).

Protocol B-1

Before beginning this protocol, check with your physician or pharmacist regarding any medications currently taken that might be causing symptoms. Remember to retake the survey after four to six weeks of following this protocol consistently.

Also, be sure to wash fruits and vegetables thoroughly in water to remove chemical residues. A safer way is to peel them when you can.

Add to your nutritional regimen

- Cabbage
- Broccoli
- Brussels sprouts
- Oranges and tangerines
- Caraway
- Dill
- Brown rice
- Barley
- Oatmeal
- Beets
- *Protocols Life Support:* Take only as directed.
- *Protocols Tea Tox and Protocols Colon Therapy:* Take two packets of each three times daily for four to six weeks.
- *Protocols Incellate:* Take one to two capsules three times daily with meals for four to six weeks.
- Drink plenty of filtered water, six to eight glasses daily to allow the body to flush toxins sufficiently.

Avoid

- Antihistamines
- Grapefruit (especially juice)

- Curcumin from spice tumeric
- Capsaicin from red chili pepper
- Clove oil
- Onions
- Perfume
- Cleaning products (bleach, ammonia, degreasers, solvents, petroleum products, aerosols)
- Permanent chemical solutions (for hair)
- Pesticides
- Foods containing MSG (read labels)
- Hair spray
- Tap water
- Over-the-counter drugs

If minimal or no improvements are seen, repeat recommendations for another four weeks.

Protocol B-2

Add to your nutritional regimen

Eat at least one of these *Group 1* foods at least once each day:

- Cabbage
- Broccoli
- Brussels sprouts
- Oranges and tangerines (no grapefruit)

Eat at least one of these *Group 2* foods at least twice each day:

- Cilantro
- Wild bear garlic
- Garlic
- Eggs

Eat at least one of these *Group 3* foods at least twice each day:

- Psyllium seed
- Oat bran
- Artichoke
- Caraway
- Dill

In addition, I recommend that you take the following supplements:

- *Protocols Life Support:* Take two packets two times daily with meals.

- *Protocols Daytime Take It Off:* Take one packet two to three times daily, twenty minutes before meals.

- *Protocols Tea Tox:* Take two packets two to three times daily between meals.

Avoid

- Antihistamines
- Grapefruit (especially juice)
- Curcumin from spice tumeric
- Capsaicin from red chili pepper
- Clove oil
- Onions
- Antiperspirants (use deodorants only)
- Cooking using aluminum cookware
- Beverages in aluminum cans
- Tap water
- Lipstick and other cosmetics
- Chewing gum or candy if dental fillings are present

Protocol B-3

Add to your nutritional regimen

- Six to eight 8-ounce glasses of water daily, preferably distilled or reverse-osmosis purified water

- After eliminating the following list of foods for a period of two weeks, rotate one food from the list back into your diet one at a time for three consecutive meals before adding the next food. If previous symptoms return or are worse, or if new symptoms begin at the addition of a particular food, you may have discovered an allergic reaction to that food. I recommend that you avoid it.

- *Protocols Life Support:* Take one packet daily.

- *Protocols Incellate:* Take one capsule three times daily with meals.

- *Protocols Cell Proof:* Take two to four capsules three times daily twenty minutes before meals.

Avoid

- Sausage
- Sauerkraut
- Tuna
- Wine
- Cheese
- Seafood
- Preserves
- Spinach
- Potatoes
- Tomatoes
- Strawberries
- Chocolate
- Bananas
- Papaya
- Nuts
- Alcohol
- Cabbage

Protocol C-4

If your responses to the health survey show you need this protocol, it will be important that you do the following:

■ Avoid damp, musty or moldy environments.

■ Buy a dehumidifier for basements.

■ Stay out of attics, old buildings, garages, storage sheds and like facilities.

Add to your nutritional regimen

■ The *Stay Healthy Diet* (page 179)

■ Psyllium or 100 percent cold pressed aloe—with no sugar added

■ *Protocols Life Support:* Take as directed.

■ *Protocols Tea Tox* and *Protocols Colon Therapy:* Take two packs of each three times daily between meals.

■ *Protocols Cell Proof:* Take two to four capsules three times daily, twenty minutes before meals.

■ *Protocols Incellate:* Take one capsule three times daily with meals.

Eliminate these foods

■ All foods containing sugar
■ Milk and other dairy products
■ Foods with high yeast or mold content (bread, cereals, grains, beer)
■ Citrus, especially juices
■ Wheat and wheat products
■ Chocolate
■ Processed and packaged foods
■ Corn and corn products (such as corn syrup)
■ Potatoes

- Tap water
- Alcoholic beverages
- Cheeses
- Dried fruits
- Melons
- Peanuts
- Rice
- Lactose sucrose

Protocol C-5

Add to your nutritional regimen

- Fiber foods (for example, oatmeal, bran, psyllium)
- The *Stay Healthy Diet* (page 179)
- *Protocols Life Support:* Take one pack one to two times daily with meals.
- *Protocols Tea Tox* and *Protocols Colon Therapy:* Take two packs of each three times daily between meals.
- *Protocols Cell Proof:* Take two to four capsules three times daily, twenty minutes before meals.

Avoid

- Raw or undercooked foods (especially meats)
- Delicatessen meats
- Handling raw meat without plastic gloves
- All processed and refined foods
- Chemical products (alcohol, solvents, pesticides, petroleum and so forth)
- Meat and dairy products older than three to four days from harvest
- Leftovers
- Tap water
- Shellfish
- Fast foods
- Contacting pets

- Putting hands into the mouth (for example, biting fingernails)
- Submersing head into swimming pools, rivers or lakes

Protocol C-6

Add to your nutritional regimen

- The *Stay Healthy Diet* (page 179)
- Raw fruits and vegetables (Don't eat fruits and vegetables at the same meal.)
- Garlic
- Chicken soup (freshly made, not from a can)
- Farm-raised meats (Commercial meats have antibiotics that lower immunity.)
- Oatmeal
- Carrot, celery, beet and garlic juice (fresh from juicer)
- Yogurt with acidophilus
- Minimum of six to eight glasses of water daily (distilled water or reverse-osmosis purified water)
- *Protocols Life Support:* Take one pack two to three times daily with meals.
- *Protocols Tea Tox* and *Protocols Colon Therapy:* Take one pack of each in the morning and in the evening.
- *Protocols Incellate:* Take one to two capsules three times daily with meals.
- *Protocols Cell Proof:* Take two to four capsules three times daily, twenty minutes before meals.

Avoid

- Sugar (and products containing sugar)
- Refined foods
- Fried foods
- Fast foods
- All sodas (naturally or artificially sweetened)

- Fruit juice (unless freshly squeezed or fresh from juicer)
- Fast food or packaged foods
- Tap water
- Small children in daycare
- Pushing to the point of exhaustion
- Extreme changes in body temperatures (from hot to cold, or cold to hot)
- Not getting enough sleep
- High stress
- Smoking

Protocol D-7

If your responses to the health survey indicate you need this protocol, you need to begin the *Protocols Keto-Diet*. (See page 183.)

- During this protocol, it is necessary to reduce fruits and vegetables significantly, which deprives the body of appropriate amounts of vitamins and minerals. Supplementation with *Protocols Life Support* will be essential in order to prevent possible deficiency.

- Also, because of the increased metabolic waste products released by the body produced due to dieting and increased protein consumption, proper cleansing must be accomplished in order to help reduce the increased workload on the liver and kidneys. The *Protocols Tea Tox* supplement will help assist in this process.

- The increased elimination of toxins ultimately overloads the colon, so the *Protocols Colon Therapy* formula helps absorb these toxins and carry them out of the body safely.

- *The Protocols Daytime Take It Off* and *Protocols Nighttime Take It Off* formulas work during this protocol by fueling the amino acid cycles that cause the body to burn fat. By fueling both cycles (daytime and nighttime), it equips the body for twenty-four-hour fat burning without feeling jittery or nervous.

Add to your nutritional regimen

Take the supplements discussed according to the following dosage during this protocol:

- *Protocols Life Support:* Take one to two packs daily with meals.
- *Protocols Tea Tox:* Take one to two packs daily between meals (morning and evening).
- *Protocols Colon Therapy:* Take one to two packs first thing in the morning.
- *Protocols Daytime Take It Off:* Take one pack twenty minutes before lunch.
- *Protocols Nighttime Take It Off:* Take one pack at bedtime on an empty stomach (no food three hours before bedtime).

Protocol D-8

If your responses to the health survey indicate you need this protocol, you need to begin the *Protocols Keto-Diet.* (See page 183.)

Add to your nutritional regimen

- Minimum of six to eight glasses of water daily (distilled water or reverse-osmosis purified water)

- *Protocols Life Support:* Take as directed.

- Exercise each day for a minimum of fifteen minutes maintaining a heart rate of between 150 and 180 beats per minute (such as aerobics, cycling, brisk walking).

Avoid

- Turnips
- Cabbage
- Mustard
- Cassava root
- Soy products
- Peanuts
- Pine nuts
- Millet
- Broccoli
- Brussels sprouts
- Cauliflower
- Kale
- Mustard greens
- Spinach

CHAPTER 16

The Stay Healthy Whole Food Diet

The basic rules for my *Stay Healthy Diet* are to eat food ONLY if it meets the following conditions:

- It comes directly from a tree or plant.
- It grows under the ground.
- It is walking, swimming or flying around.
- It is not forbidden by the Bible.

This diet eliminates destructive eating habits and offers us a healthy lifestyle based on the perfect provision of God. In order to enjoy health, we have to avoid the chemical-infested, refined, nutrient-deficient, dead foods and fill our bodies with whole foods that are full of life and vital nutrients.

Nutritional Regimen

Add to your nutritional regimen

- Eat whole foods as they exist in nature before man's intervention.

- Eat a wide variety of foods, including vegetables, fruits, grains, dairy and meat.

- Do no overeat even good foods. See the *Hand-Size Diet Food List* on page 181 for proper portions.

- Drink at least five 8-ounce glasses of water daily. (Avoid chlorinated sources.)

Avoid

- Refined foods
- Canned or packaged foods
- Processed foods
- Sugar
- Alcohol
- Fried foods
- Partially hydrogenated foods and oils
- Margarine or spreads (use butter instead)
- White breads, white rice and so forth
- Preservatives

Tip: To shop for foods on the *Stay Healthy Diet,* stay around the outside perimeter of your grocery store. That is where most stores stock whole foods: fruits, vegetables, meats, dairy and so forth. The middle aisles are full of altered foods.

Dietary rules

- Don't eat when you are not hungry.

- Don't worry about calories.

- Eat enough food that you are not hungry, but stop eating as soon as you are satisfied.

- Eat no refined or packaged foods.

- Slow down while eating; take time to chew.

- Maintain a minimum consumption of five 8-ounce glasses of water daily.

Final Comments

- Determine that it is time to address any bondage you have to food.

- Understand that you were not designed to live to eat; you can have health only if you eat to live.

- When you become personally responsible for your diet, your body will reward you with health and more energy.

- Get the *concept*; be *consistent*; stay *committed*.

HAND-SIZE DIET FOOD LIST

Choose a portion from each category (proteins, carbohydrates and vegetables) to make a meal. Add a serving of vegetables to at least two of your daily meals. A portion is about the size of your hand. If you are a small person with small hands, your portion is smaller than the portion for a person that may be larger than you.

Proteins

Chicken breast	Lean ham	Shrimp
Turkey breast	Lean ground turkey	Crab
Lean New York strip	Veal	Fish
Lean ground beef	Lamb	Lobster
Top sirloin steak	Venison	Any "lean" meat
Top round steak		

AVOID sausage, dried beef, hot dogs, Vienna sausage or potted meat.

Canned tuna and chicken can be used, but the less you use canned meat, the better.

Use butter and other condiments sparingly.

Carbohydrates

Baked potato	Steamed wild rice	Melon
Sweet potato	Pasta	Apple
Yam	Oatmeal	Orange
Squash	Barley	Strawberries
Pumpkin	Beans	Whole-wheat bread
Steamed brown rice	Corn	Fat- and sugar-free yogurt

Vegetables

Lettuce	Green peppers	Beets
Tomato	Chinese cabbage	Greens
Carrots	Sauerkraut	Summer squash
Peas	Bean sprouts	Okra
Artichoke	Water chestnuts	Broccoli
Cabbage	Snow pea pods	Onions
Celery	Bamboo shoots	Turnips
Cucumber	Kohlrabi	Peppers
Asparagus	Spinach	Kale
Cauliflower	Chard	Rhubarb
String beans	Mushrooms	Zucchini
Green beans		

CHAPTER 17

Protocols Keto-Diet

To help break an addictive, destructive and out-of-balance habitual eating pattern, many health practitioners recommend a ketogenic diet. The ketogenic diet has been around since the 1700s and used to be the treatment of choice for diabetics. Most recently it has been made popular by Dr. Atkins and others as a method for weight loss.

The addictive-eating pattern usually consists mainly in the consumption of carbohydrates, especially the refined ones. These are foods that either contain or metabolize in the system as sugars. When the body burns sugar primarily as fuel instead of fat, as we discussed, an array of health problems will result, including gaining unnecessary weight.

This diet is designed to change your destructive way of eating. If you are abusing carbohydrates, the obvious way to "fix" it is to eliminate or reduce the additive substance. The way to do this is to avoid the foods that contain carbohydrates and eat foods that do not. It's that simple!

The ketogenic diet is not meant to be followed indefinitely. It is helpful to the point that desired weight loss is achieved and health has been restored by breaking the "carboholic addiction." At that point, I recommend that you move to the *Stay Healthy*

Hand-Portion Diet to maintain the body's newly achieved balance. (See page 181.)

Low-Carbohydrate Foods

Listed below are foods that are acceptable for the ketogenic diet because they contain no carbohydrates, or only a minimal amount.

List A—Meats

EAT any fish, fowl, beef, pork, lamb, veal, ham or venison.

AVOID canned, processed, battered and fried meats.

AVOID shellfish, sausage, dried beef, hot dogs, Vienna sausage, potted or canned meat.

CHOOSE lean cuts and trim away fat.

List B—Eggs

Omelets	Scrambled	Soft-boiled
Hard-boiled	Deviled	Poached

List C—Cheeses

4 ounces of any hard and aged cheese
Aged and fresh cheese
Mozzarella
Swiss
Cheddar
Cream cheese (sparingly)
Cow and goat cheese
AVOID processed cheese and cheese spreads.

List D—Salad greens

Lettuce	Cucumbers	Chives
Arugula	Alfalfa sprouts	Celery
Parsley	Fennel mushrooms	Escarole
Endive	Romaine	Sorrel
Chickory	Radicchio	Peppers and olives

List E—Vegetables

Asparagus	Greens	Cabbage
Chinese cabbage	Summer squash	Chard
Sauerkraut	Okra	Broccoli
Avocado	Pumpkin	Onions
Brussels sprouts	Snow pea pods	Turnips
Water chestnuts	Bamboo shoots	Peppers
Squash	Kohlrabi	Kale
Mushrooms	Spinach	Rhubarb
String beans	Bean sprouts	Zucchini
Beets		

Beverage list

Water
Club soda
Mineral water
Beef or chicken bouillon

Decaffeinated tea or coffee (to avoid possible blood sugar reactions from caffeine, limit regular coffee and tea consumption to three cups daily)

Condiments/oils

Use these condiments and oils freely; they will not bring you out of ketosis.

Salt	Horseradish	Vinegar
Pepper	Mustard	

Vanilla and other extracts

Dry powdered spice that contains no sugar

Real butter (no margarine or spreads)
Flax oil
Extra-virgin olive oil
Canola oil
Mayonnaise

Instructions for the Protocols Keto-Diet

For the first week, eat only foods from lists A, B and C, along with less than 1 cup loosely packed salad once or twice daily from list D.

Go to your local drug store and buy some Ketostix in order to determine when you body goes into ketosis. Ketosis is the process that involves the body breaking down fat into ketone bodies, which will be used for fuel in place of carbohydrates. It usually begins between the second and fourth day of the Keto-Diet. When you reach this point, the Ketostix will turn purple when tested in a sample of urine. During your Keto-Diet you want your body to remain in ketosis. The darker the purple, the less hunger and cravings you will have.

After remaining in full ketosis for two weeks, you can slowly add vegetables from list E back into your diet. Start by adding ¼ cup of one vegetable with each meal. Continue testing your urine with Ketostix through this process. If the Ketostix no longer turns purple, it means you have added back too many carbohydrates. If this happens, simply eat less of the vegetables on list E. Test your urine again in two days. When purple color has returned, then you are back in ketosis. In this way you will find your body's *balance point*. Your goal is to add back as many vegetables as you can, yet still remain in ketosis. It's that simple!

The average carboholic addition takes approximately eight to twelve weeks to break. Some people may want to continue for longer periods of time in order to lose greater amounts of weight. If you choose to remain on this diet for longer periods of time, I always recommend that you be monitored by a physician. Any person should be monitored by a physician when losing significant amounts of weight.

RULES FOR THE KETO-DIET

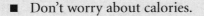

- Don't worry about calories.

- Don't eat when you are not hungry.

- Eat only enough food to satisfy your hunger.

- Eat no refined or packaged foods.

- Slow down while eating, and take time to chew.

- If you find yourself getting weak or fatigued during the Keto-Diet, you may be electrolyte depleted. Add some salt to your diet, as well as some parsley, watercress or other high-potassium foods. Though bananas are a high-potassium food, do not eat them because they will bring you out of ketosis.

- Fruits are very high in carbohydrates. If any are eaten on the diet, you should only have them with one meal per day and only a couple of times per week. Otherwise, they will tend to bring you out of ketosis.

- Maintain a minimum consumption of six to eight glasses of water daily. Avoid tap water.

- Don't forget to exercise at least twenty minutes daily, maintaining a heart rate of 150 to 170 beats per minute. The objective is to work up a sweat. This exercise can consist of walking, running or jumping in place.

- Take the *Protocols* supplements recommended in Protocol D-7. (See page 176.)

What About Prescription Medications?

Certain medications slow down the weight-loss process. These include thorazine, sparine, mellaril, prednisone, female hormones, testosterone, birth control pills as well as long-term antidepressants. Weight loss may be slower if you are taking these medications. If this becomes a problem, you may want to discuss it with your physician.

If you have a thyroid problem, you will also have slower weight loss. This is one of the reasons I recommend that a routine physical be performed by a physician before starting any diet.

Note: It is not uncommon to experience a few days of feeling bad initially when you begin the Keto-Diet. You may experience withdrawal symptoms from carbohydrates as your metabolism changes from a sugar-burning to a fat-burning process. Your symptoms should only last a couple of days. If they last longer, check with your physician.

The Top Ten Questions

The information that follows are answers to the most common ten questions I am asked in my clinical practice. I have tried to answer them as completely as possible in this section and at least give you some basis for your decisions.

QUESTION 1:
WHAT ABOUT CALCIUM SUPPLEMENTS?

A lot of people ask me what type of calcium they should take, sometimes referring to coral calcium or oyster shell calcium. I like to answer them with a simple question: "Have you ever seen anyone chewing on a piece of coral or on an oyster shell?" I am not saying those sources of calcium won't work; I am just responding with common sense based on the way we were designed. Plant sources of calcium such as calcium citrates, malates and aspartates are my personal preference. Perhaps if we were designed with a beak like a chicken, I would prefer the other sources for calcium.

QUESTION 2:
IS COLLOIDAL SUSPENSION THE MOST ABSORBABLE FORM OF MINERALS?

Colloidal suspension is the term used for the process of live plants drawing minerals from the soil and suspending them into their plant solutions. Because it is the natural design for absorbing minerals, it is the best form.

However, some of the minerals on the market that claim to be in colloidal suspension are not processed in this way. Some claim there were glacier ice minerals that flooded fields of a certain geographical area and that the plants growing in that area were heavily saturated with mineral deposits.

Often there is a discrepancy in the process used to extract their mineral solutions. They dig up the dead prehistoric swamp grass and grind it up into a solution and call it colloidal suspension. It is not a true colloidal suspension like that of the vitamins, citrates, malates and aspartates that are extracted from live plants. Remember! Watch out for fad, hype and claims of product superiority.

QUESTION 3:
SHOULD I TAKE MORE CALCIUM TO PREVENT OSTEOPOROSIS?

Osteoporosis is not caused by not taking enough calcium supplementation. It is usually caused from an acidic diet of too much sugar, refined foods, coffee, tea, soda and nicotine. The body draws calcium out of the bones (calcium phosphate) in order to buffer the excess acids in the system.

When the body begins drawing calcium out of bones faster than it can metabolize it, osteoporosis begins. Besides changing your lifestyle to a more healthy diet, the way to increase calcium metabolism is to increase weight resistance training. To do weightlifting against some type of physical resistance, you do not have to use heavy weights. It simply needs to be consistent, a maximum of three times weekly for at least twenty to thirty minutes, working the entire body. This weight resistance exercise places a demand on the bones, causing them to ask the body for more calcium, thus strengthening the bones.

It is important to remember that taking too much calcium can cause as much harm to the body as the right amount can bring benefit. Balance and human design are the way to go.

QUESTION 4:
ARE THERE NATURAL WAYS TO HELP BLOOD PRESSURE PROBLEMS?

The three most common types of blood pressure problems I see in clinical practice are portal (liver), renal (kidney) and stress induced (adrenal).

A basic screening you can do in the home to find out which area is causing your blood pressure problem is to follow this simple protocol:

- Take blood pressure at the same time each day.
- Take it sitting in the same chair.
- Let the same person take it each time.
- Use the same arm consistently.

Day 1 (screening for high blood pressure caused from an acidic system)

- **Step 1:** Take your blood pressure, and record results. If the blood pressure is high, take 500 milligrams of magnesium and potassium supplement (a combined formula is preferred).

- **Step 2:** Wait fifteen minutes after taking the supplement, and then take your blood pressure again.

If your blood pressure dropped by five or more points, then one of the contributing factors to the problem is the body is being stressed from an *acidic condition of the system.*

Day 2 (screening for high blood pressure caused from adrenal stress)

- **Step 1:** Take your blood pressure while lying flat on your back, and record the results.

- **Step 2:** Before removing the cuff, immediately stand up and take your blood pressure again in the standing position. Once again record the results.

If your blood pressure dropped five or more points upon standing, it is an indication that the *adrenal glands are stressed.*

Day 3 (screening for high blood pressure caused from renal [kidney] and/or portal [liver] stress)

- **Step 1:** Take your blood pressure, and record the results. If your blood pressure is high, take one packet (four capsules) of Tea Tox (or other herbal liver/kidney detox).

- **Step 2:** Wait fifteen minutes after taking Tea Tox capsules, and take your blood pressure again.

If your blood pressure dropped five or more points, then one of the contributing factors to the problem is *liver/kidney stress.*

Recommendations

- *Acidic system:* Take 500 milligrams of magnesium and potassium three times per day with meals. Also, increase alkaline substances in the diet (fruits and green vegetables, especially in their raw form).

- *Adrenal stress:* You need to supplement for adrenal support with pantothenic acid, adrenal glandulars and ginseng taken three times daily. You can usually find these in combination formulas labeled adrenal support. Work to reduce emotional stress, and use relaxation techniques and aerobic exercise.

- *Liver/kidney stress:* Filter cleansing is a must, using a natural liver/kidney (detox) cleansing formula. I recommend using Tea Tox, two packs three times per day between meals.

Some may have one, two or all three of these hypertension conditions combined. These conditions need to be tested for individually and monitored periodically, perhaps every couple of days initially, then weekly.

After approximately six weeks, if your blood pressure has regulated, then cut dosages to one time daily for maintenance.

Anyone who has high blood pressure should avoid tobacco products, coffee, black tea, sugar, sodas and caffeine.

QUESTION 5:
IS IT OK TO USE ARTIFICIAL SWEETENERS?

Most products that contain artificial sweeteners use terms such as "diet" or "contains no sugar." This terminology is commonly used on labels of soft drinks, for example. I can express my answer by highlighting the first three letters—D-I-E—of the word *diet*. That is a pretty good synopsis of how these artificial sweetener "poisons" affect your body. NutraSweet is a known neurotoxin, affecting the brain and central nervous system, and has been linked with a host of diseases and neural disorders. The pink packs speak for themselves; they are labeled with a warning as a possible cause of cancer written on the back of them. Christians use these cancer-causing agents every day, while many chide others who smoke cigarettes.

If you want to use natural sweeteners, I highly recommend the herbal extract *Stevia*. It does not produce insulin reactions and has been used safely for thousands of years. I have used it myself for a number of years and have recommended it to many of my patients. If you are having trouble finding something good to drink, you might try squeezing half a lemon in an 8-ounce glass of water and sweetening it with Stevia to taste. It's a great glass of lemonade, and it's actually good for you.

If you are looking for a sugarless gum, do not use a product sweetened with aspartame or any other chemical sweetener; they are known to cause damage to cells, especially brain cells. Find a brand that uses xylitol. It slowly digests in the human body (about one-fifth as fast as glucose), so it doesn't cause a rapid rise in blood sugar. The bacteria that produce dental decay cannot use it as a substrate, so it actually promotes dental health from that standpoint.

QUESTION 6:
IS IT OK TO TAKE TYLENOL FOR A HEADACHE?

The reason you have a headache is not because your body is low on Tylenol. Consider a more "natural" treatment that deals with the cause of your headache and doesn't simply mask the symptom.

QUESTION 7:
CAN NATURAL MEDICINE TREAT LUPUS, RHEUMATOID ARTHRITIS, CANCER AND OTHER LIFE-THREATENING DISEASES?

It is important to remember that we do not treat disease; we treat the body to promote health. After establishing a healthy lifestyle of diet and exercise, we can add supplementation that will support the body's defense system. By feeding the cells to make them healthy *(Protocols Life Support)*, cleansing the filters to remove the poisons that cause cell damage *(Protocols Tea Tox)* and protecting the cell from oxidation and damage *(Protocols Incellate)*, the body can reproduce healthy cells, eventually producing a healthy body. Sick people produce sick cells; that is why they are sick. We treat the body on a cellular level; we do not treat disease.

QUESTION 8:
DO LOW-FAT, NONFAT FOODS HELP YOU LOSE WEIGHT AND LOWER CHOLESTEROL?

Most low-fat, nonfat foods are extremely high in refined sugars. Sugar is the cause of weight gain, not fat. It also elevates cholesterol. Sugar stimulates the release of insulin, which causes the body to store fat, resulting in elevated cholesterol.

QUESTION 9:
WHAT TYPES OF FOOD SHOULD WE EAT?

Here are some rules of thumb for choosing the right foods:

- Eat whole foods (natural foods that have not been altered) as often as possible.

- Drink water instead of coffee, tea, sodas and other drinks.

- The best way to shop for food is on the outside perimeter of the grocery store. That is where you will find all of your whole foods: meats, dairy, bread, fruits and vegetables. When you have done that, *go home!* Everything on the other aisles is sliced, diced, chunked, cooked and ground foods with chemicals added.

QUESTION 10:
IS IT OK TO EAT SHELLFISH?

Shellfish are basically water filters, cleaning up the debris in the waters where they live. Thousands of gallons of raw sewage are being dumped into our oceans every day. Guess who is cleaning it up? Shellfish.

Imagine putting clean water into a swimming pool and dumping sewage into it from one end. Then place all kinds of fish into the pool. The ones that swim toward the sewage end will be cleaning it up; they are the ones to avoid. Shellfish would be swimming toward the sewage. If you decide to eat shellfish in spite of these grim facts, make sure you have plenty of breath mints.

Comparison of Education for Chiropractic Physician and Medical Doctor

COMPARISONS OF THE OVERALL CURRICULUM STRUCTURE FOR CHIROPRACTIC AND MEDICAL SCHOOLS[1]

HOURS	Chiropractic Schools		Medical Schools	
	MEAN	PERCENTAGE	MEAN	PERCENTAGE
Total Contact	4822	100%	4667	100%
Basic science	1416	29%	1200	26%
Clinical science	3406	71%	3467	74%
Chiropractic science	1975	41%	0	0
Clerkship	1405	29%	3467	74%

COMPARISONS OF HOURS OF BASIC SCIENCES
EDUCATION IN MEDICAL AND CHIROPRACTIC [2]

SUBJECT	Chiropractic Schools		Medical Schools	
	HOURS	% OF TOTAL	HOURS	% OF TOTAL
Anatomy	570	40	368	31
Biochemistry	150	11	120	10
Microbiology	120	8	120	10
Public Health	70	5	289	24
Physiology	305	21	142	12
Pathology	205	14	162	14
Total Hours	1,420	100	1,200	100

What Vitamins Should I Take?

For over a decade I have been involved in research and development for nutritional product formulation. Over the years I have seen many nutritional supplements come and go. Many of these products promise to heal everything from cancer to athlete's foot. Since nutritional products cannot be patented, it became very popular to create a gimmick to sell the product, especially something spooky, mystical or ancient that had been kept a secret for thousands of years.

Another popular fad is what I call "cookbook" nutrition. People prescribe nutrients instead of drugs to treat symptoms. For example, they recommend B complex for stress or feverfew for migraine headaches. Although there are times when these kinds of recommendations can be useful, basically this approach to healthcare is not much different from conventional healthcare that treats symptoms without addressing the cause of the problem. The only difference is that nutrients have replaced drugs. I believe it makes more sense to supplement the needs of the whole body rather than trying to single out certain symptoms for treatment.

When I first started formulating nutritional products, I knew that our bodies needed added vitamins, minerals, essential fatty acids, amino acids and enzymes. At that time I thought that the more you took, the better. I started recommending that people take handfuls of vitamins. I would try to put everything but the kitchen sink into my "multi-pack" vitamin. Some people's conditions did improve, but the conditions of others grew worse.

As I progressed in my understanding, the next phase I went through was recommending that all my patients cleanse their systems. I had all my patients detoxing the liver, colon, kidneys and blood and using every other type of cleansing compound imaginable. Some patients' conditions improved, but the conditions of others grew worse.

Finally, after years of experience and thousands of patients' visits, I realized that when I had patients cleansing their systems at the same time I gave vitamins, minerals, amino acids, essential fatty acids and enzyme supplements, most of my patients seemed to respond positively. I began to understand that cleansing the body removed the toxins that were competing for the nutrient sites in the cells. That facilitated the nutrients' absorption by the body, and less nutrients were needed because of increased absorption.

Through all of my trial and error to learn the right protocols to recommend, I have been able to formulate a system that has improved thousands of patients, both locally and across the nation. My partner, Lanny Shepard, is a six-time national, one-time world, all-natural power lifting champion. When I first met Lanny, I discovered he was quite knowledgeable regarding nutrition and was taking many supplements. In spite of that, he still had a lot of health problems.

We decided to form a nutritional company, which we called PROTOCOLS, Inc. Of course, Lanny began to take my nutritional supplements. Happily, Lanny is now one of the healthiest people I know. His health problems have disappeared, and he still enjoys working out, quite strenuously, at his health club.

I was motivated to begin this nutritional product company because for years I had seen people purchase supplements by the bagful, but they had no protocol, no systematic plan for supplementing their whole body. I began to develop scientific protocols that were based on individual need, with recommendations for lifestyle changes to help the products work to greater advantage. I tell my patients that nutrition and the way the body responds to it has not changed since the Garden of Eden. Plants still absorb minerals from the soil, and sunlight hits the plant, causing photosynthesis to produce vitamins. We eat the plants and get the nutrients. That is God's design. The problem is that because of the deterioration of the planet, the soils are becoming more and more depleted.

Is soil depletion a reality? It is common knowledge today that our soil is severely lacking in nutrients; that is why farmers spend millions of dollars on chemical fertilizers to help grow their plants. Adding to that the increasing population that places dramatic stress on the land to overproduce, we have a global problem of trying to grow crops that have adequate nutrients. This is why I believe we have to participate in some type of nutrient supplementation to insure health.

As I have mentioned, I believe that natural medicine should be *primary healthcare* medicine. The combinations of natural supplements and herbs listed below have taken years for me to modify and perfect. Having developed a comprehensive supplementation system called *Protocols, Inc.,* I can report that thousands of people have seen tremendous improvements in their health from taking these supplement combinations.

I personally take these supplements every day of my life. If you are like me, you are ready for something that is easy to take, yet gives comprehensive supplementation for all your health needs. If you take our entire *primary healthcare system,* you will not need to take additional supplements; you will be getting all the nutrients your body needs for health.

Our complete supplement system is a comprehensive, nutrient-providing, herbal-cleansing protocol that helps the body to cope with the challenges of everyday life. We have prepared nutrient and herbal combinations and placed them into separate, individual, pre-dosed packets for your convenience.

These supplements are both safe and effective, yet they are also convenient and affordable. By taking these products regularly, along with proper lifestyle choices of exercising and eating a proper diet, you'll begin to experience more energy and a sense of well-being. And you will have the satisfaction of knowing you are doing an excellent job of maintaining the body that God has given you.

Protocol 1—Life Support

Remember the mandate for your health that requires you to *feed the cell*. Through our company, Protocols, Inc., I have developed a supplement called *Life Support*, which contains the proper balance of vitamins, minerals, essential fatty acids, enzymes, antioxidants and other vital nutrients to supplement your diet. It is essentially a potent multivitamin-mineral supplement. *Life Support* works in your body as fertilizer works for grass, strengthening and enhancing health.

The key to any supplementation protocol is achieving the proper balance as well as proper ratios of nutrients. I have formulated the *Life Support* nutrient packets so that they are comprehensive in content as well as convenient to take. They should be taken with meals once or twice daily. On the days that your schedule is more demanding, you may want to take two packets a day to assure maximum energy. On the days that are less demanding, you may only require one packet.

When most people start taking supplements initially, they feel significant increases in energy levels as well as a wonderful sense of well-being. Do not be surprised if many of your unpleasant symptoms begin to diminish simply as a result of taking nutritional therapy. The idea is to offer the body all the nutrients it needs so that it can perform all its healing functions.

Protocol 2—Tea Tox

Cleansing and protecting the cell, as we discussed, is also important to your health. We have developed a combination of herbal preparations that accomplishes the tasks of cleansing, repairing and protecting the cells. The product's name is *Tea Tox*. The herbal compounds used in this product are listed in the *Physician's Desk Reference of Herbal Medicines* as well as the *Herbal German Monographs,* which provide scientific evidence and research that support their health claims. The particular combinations used in Tea Tox were derived from many years of objective findings reported in clinical practice and not by scientific research alone.

Colon Therapy

Our herbal product *Colon Therapy* safely and gently cleanses the bowel without the use of any herbal laxatives. It also coats and lubricates the bowel, which helps transit time to prevent carcinogens from being held against the colon wall. The ingredients contained are shown to remove the toxins that cause many allergies, which people experience today, as well as killing yeast and bad bacteria. It also has nutrients that help cleanse the upper GI tract and increase its secretions. It helps to heal the complete digestive system. It contains probiotics, or good bacteria, that are necessary to help digest food and that act as the first line of defense in your body's immune system.

Protocol 3—Incellate

It is also necessary to protect your cells from destructive forces. We have discussed the benefits of antioxidant therapy—remember the apple and rusty metal that were oxidized? Antioxidants prevent oxidation from breaking down your cells and making them vulnerable for attachment of radicals. *Incellate* is one of the strongest antioxidant products on the market. It has a full range of antioxidants from the finest sources available. Protect your cells from damage by taking Incellate on a regular basis. You owe it to your body.

Cell Proof

Cell Proof was formulated to help assist the body in strengthening the immune system. It contains medicinal mushrooms along with compounds called ellagitannins that have been used successfully for thousands of years by various cultures. More recently these compounds have been shown by scientific studies to be extremely effective ancillary treatments for ailments ranging from cancer to HIV. Anyone who wants to strengthen his immune system should benefit from taking this product. Many people who have had chronic degenerative conditions, including cancer, have reported a significant increase in energy and overall well-being while taking *Cell Proof* in combination with *Incellate* at doses as high as four capsules of each product taken three times daily.

Protocol 4—Take It Off (Daytime and Nighttime)

If you stick your hand in a bowl of lard and pull it out, you will have a mess on your hands. If you rinse them under a faucet of water, you will have a bigger mess. Why? Lard or fat is not water-soluble. However, you can take dishwashing soap or another type of fat emulsifier, and it will break the fat down and clean it off your hands.

In this same way, blood is water-soluble, and fat does not break down in the blood unless it comes into contact with some type of emulsifier. The *Daytime* and *Nighttime Take It Off* formulas work to break down the fats in the blood so they can be used by the body for fuel instead of being stored. Because of its mechanism of action, it can also be used as an oral chelation program.

If you are ready to improve the quality of your life, contact Hannen Health Care Clinic for more information. You may call 334-393-9355 or 1-866-DOC-SAYS. Please visit our website at www.DOCTALKS.com to begin the protocol that will change your life forever.

NOTES

Chapter 1
The Wonder of Human Design

1. The National Center for Health Statistics, Division of Data Services, 3311 Toledo Road, Hyattsville, MD 20782. Phone, (301) 458-4636; e-mail, nchsqery@CDC.gov.

Chapter 2
How Do We Get Sick?

1. W. A. Newman Dorland, ed., *Dorland's Illustrated Medical Dictionary* (Philadelphia: W. B. Saunders Co., 2000).

Chapter 3
A Society of Carboholics

1. The National Center for Health Statistics, Division of Data Services, 3311 Toledo Road, Hyattsville, MD 20782. Phone, (301) 458-4636; e-mail, nchsqery@CDC.gov.
2. National Diabetes Statistics, General information and national estimates on diabetes in the United States, 2000. National Diabetes Information Clearinghouse, a service of the National Institute of Diabetes and Digestive and Kidney Diseases (NIDDK), a part of the National Institutes of Health (NIH). Source retrieved from the Internet on April 10, 2003 at www.niddk.nih.gov/health/diabetes/pubs.dmstats/dmstats.htm.
3. Food Personality Profiles: Carboholic, retrieved from the Internet at http://weightdefense.isishops.com/profiles_carboholic.aspx.
4. Jim Barlow, "Consuming more protein, fewer carbohydrates may be healthier," News Bureau University of Illinois at Urbana-Champaign (April 1, 2001): retrieved from the Internet at www.news.uicuc.edu/scitips/01/04diet.html.
5. Kelly D. Brownell and David S. Ludwig, "Fighting Obesity and the Food Lobby," *The Washington Post* (June 9, 2002): B7. Retrieved from the Internet at Washington Post Archives, www.washingtonpost.com.
6. Ibid.

Chapter 4
America's Worst Killer Diseases

1. The National Center for Health Statistics, Division of Data Services, 3311 Toledo Road, Hyattsville, MD 20782. Phone, (301) 458-4636; e-mail, nchsqery@CDC.gov.
2. Bernard W. Stewart and Paul Kleihues, eds., *World Cancer Report* (Lyon, France: International Agency for Research on Cancer, World Health Organization, 2003).

Chapter 5
Feed the Cell

1. Thomas Perneger, Paul Whelton and Michael Klag, "Risk of Kidney Failure Associated With the Use of Acetaminophen, Aspirin and Nonsteroidal Anti-Inflammatory Drugs," *The New England Journal of Medicine* 331 (25) (December 22, 1994): 1675–1679.
1. Sheldon Saul Hendler, M.D., Ph.D., *The Doctors' Vitamin and Minerals Encyclopedia* (New York: Simon and Schuster, 1990), 250–251.
2. Dr. Edward Howell, *Food Enzymes for Health and Longevity,* 2nd edition (n.p.: Lotus Press, 1994).

Chapter 6
Cleanse and Protect the Cell

1. Rita Rubin, "Smog Clouds Nation's Health," *USA Today* (May 23, 2000).
2. Hendler, *The Doctors' Vitamin and Minerals Encyclopedia,* 315.
3. Jill Doughterty, "Soviet Anthrax Accident Killed 60" (October 16, 2001): retrieved from the Internet at www.cnn.com/2001/WORLD/europe/10/16/russia.anthrax.index.html.
4. E. Negri et al., "Intake of selected micronutrients and the risk of breast cancer," *Int J Cancer* 65 (1996): 140–144. A. M. Nomura et al., "Serum vitamin levels and the risk of cancer of specific sites in men of Japanese ancestry in Hawaii," *Cancer Res* 45 (1985): 2369–2372. G. S. Omenn, "Chemoprevention of lung cancer: the rise and demise of beta carotene," *Annu Rev Public Health* 19 (1998): 73–79. P. R. Palan et al., "Plasma levels of antioxidant beta carotene and alpha-tocopherol in uterine cervix dysplasias and cancer," *Nutr Cancer* 15 (1991): 13–20. N. Potischman et al., "Breast cancer and dietary and plasma concentrations of carotenoids and vitamin A," *Am J Clin Nut* 52 (1990): 909–915.

5. G. S. Omenn, G. Goodman, M. Thornquist et al., "The beta carotene and retinal efficacy trial (caret) for chemoprevention of lung cancer in high risk populations, smokers and asbestos-exposed workers," *Cancer* Res 54 (1994): 2038S–2043S.
6. Joseph E. Pizzorno Jr., N.D. and Michael T. Murray, N.D., eds., *Textbook of Natural Medicine,* 2nd ed. (New York: Churchill Livingstone, 1999), 484.
7. "Grape seed proanthocyanidins improved cardiac recovery during reperfusion after ischemia in isolated rat hearts," *The American Journal of Clinical Nutrition* 75(5) (May 2002): 894–899.

Chapter 7
Hormone "HELP!"

1. Dorland, ed., *Dorland's Illustrated Medical Dictionary,* s.v. "hormone."
2. Arthur C. Guyton, M.D. and John E. Hall, *Textbook of Medical Physiology,* 10th ed. (Philadelphia: W. B. Saunders Co., 2000), 836.
3. Ibid.
4. Majid Ali, M.D., "Chemical Conflict: The Age of Estrogen Overdrive," *Lifespanner* (December 1994).
5. Raquel Martin with Judi Gerstung, D.C., *The Estrogen Alternative: Natural Hormone Therapy with Botanical Progesterone* (Rochester, VT: Healing Arts Press, 2000).
6. Leta Lee, "Estrogen, Progesterone, and Female Problems," *Earth Letter* vol. I , 2 (June 1991).
7. Niels H. Lauersen, M.D., *PMS: Premenstrual Syndrome and You* (New York: Simon and Schuster, 1983).
8. Martin, *The Estrogen Alternative.*
9. Raymond Peat, *Progesterone in Orthomolecular Medicine* (Eugene, OR: Raymond Peat, Ph.D., 2001).
10. John R. Lee, "The Estrogen Question," *The John R. Lee, M.D. Medical Letter* (November 1998).
12. Martin, *The Estrogen Alternative.*

Chapter 8
Design for Beating Stress

1. *Taber's Cyclopedic Medical Dictionary,* 18th ed. (Philadelphia, PA: F. A. Davis Company, 1993), s.v. "stress," "stressor."
2. Pizzorno and Murray, eds., *Textbook of Natural Medicine.*
3. Ibid.

Chapter 9
Design for Beating Depression

1. *Funk and Wagnalls Standard Desk Dictionary,* vol. 2 (n.p.: Funk and Wagnalls Company, 1980), s.v. "suppression."
2. Russell L. Blaylock, *Excitotoxins: The Taste That Kills* (Santa Fe, NM: Health Press, 1997).
3. *Oxford American Dictionary* (n.p.: Oxford University Press, 2001), s.v. "oppress."
4. Dorland, ed., *Dorland's Illustrated Medical Dictionary,* s.v. "depression."

Chapter 10
Evaluating Your Belief System

1. *Taber's Cyclopedic Medical Dictionary,* s.v. "Hippocratic oath."
2. Walter D. Glanze and Kenneth N. Anderson, eds., *Mosby's Medical Encyclopedia* (New York: Signet Books, 1998), s.v. "Aesculapius."
3. *Nelson's Bible Dictionary,* retrieved from PC Bible Software, Version 1.4B, copyright © 1993, 1994, s.v. "physician."
4. James Strong, ed., *The New Strong's Exhaustive Concordance of the Bible* (Nashville: Thomas Nelson, 1997), s.v. "pharmakeia."

Chapter 11
Faith and Divine Healing

1. *Oxford American Dictionary,* s.v. "faith."
2. F. F. Bosworth, *Christ the Healer* (Grand Rapids, MI: Fleming H. Revell, 2001).
3. Ibid.

Chapter 13
Designed As Peculiar Treasure

1. Strong, *The New Strong's Exhaustive Concordance of the Bible,* "peculiar."

Appendix B
Comparison of Education for Chiropractic Physician and Medical Doctor

1. Center for Studies in Health Policy, Inc., Washington, DC. Personal communication of 1995 unpublished data from Meredith Gonyea, Ph.D. Used by permission.
2. Source retrieved from the Internet: www.chiroweb.com/archives/ahcpr/chapter3.htm. Used by permission.